HARD-CORE ROMANCE

D1257419

HARD-CORE ROMANCE

Fifty Shades of Grey, Best-Sellers, and Society

EVA ILLOUZ

The University of Chicago Press Chicago and London

EVA ILLOUZ is professor at the Hebrew University in Jerusalem and president of the Bezalel Academy of Arts and Design. She is the author of seven books, most recently of *Why Love Hurts*.

The University of Chicago Press, Chicago 60637
The University of Chicago Press, Ltd., London
© 2014 by Eva Illouz
All rights reserved. Published 2014.
Printed in the United States of America

23 22 21 20 19 18 17 16 15 14   1 2 3 4 5

ISBN-13: 978-0-226-15341-4 (cloth)
ISBN-13: 978-0-226-15369-8 (paper)
ISBN-13: 978-0-226-15355-1 (e-book)
DOI: 10.7208/chicago/9780226153551.001.0001

Originally published as *Die neue Liebesordnung. Frauen, Männer und "Shades of Grey."* © Suhrkamp Verlag Berlin 2013.

Library of Congress Cataloging-in-Publication Data

Illouz, Eva, 1961– author.
    [Neue Liebesordnung. English]
    Hard-core romance : Fifty shades of Grey, best-sellers, and society / Eva Illouz.
        pages cm
    "Originally published as Die neue Liebesordnung : Frauen, Männer und 'Shades of Grey.' © Suhrkamp Verlag Berlin 2013" — Title page verso.
    Includes bibliographical references and index.
    ISBN 978-0-226-15341-4 (cloth : alkaline paper) — ISBN 978-0-226-15369-8 (paperback : alkaline paper) — ISBN 978-0-226-15355-1 (e-book) 1. James, E. L. Fifty shades of Grey. 2. Erotic literature— Social aspects. 3. Best sellers—Social aspects. I Title.
    HQ462.I45 2014
    808.8'03538—dc23

                                                          2013046331

CONTENTS

ACKNOWLEDGMENTS

This book was written with respect and suspicion for popular cultural forms. Many persons have helped me circle around this respect and suspicion with care. The incomparable Eva Gilmer and Heinrich Geiselberger thought of it first. Dana Kaplan and Daniel Gilon helped me with some crucial bibliographical additions and fresh insights on sexuality. Dipesh Chakrabarty, who makes friendship into a work of art, convinced me to take this book to the North American continent. Susan Neiman, whose depth and loyalty have been essential additions to my life, has offered crucial comments with her usual brilliance. Two anonymous reviewers for the University of Chicago Press generously and insightfully helped redress the weaknesses of the manuscript. Finally, Alan Thomas at the University of Chicago Press must be thanked wholeheartedly for displaying the unusual mix of enthusiasm, efficiency, and intellectual rigor that make his publishing house stellar.

HARD-CORE ROMANCE

1 / Best-Sellers and Our Social Unconscious

Those of us who think that modernity has marked significant progress in the human condition can take stock of the differences that separate "us" (moderns) from "them" (members of premodern societies) by invoking fast trains, frozen food, or vaccines; or better, the right to vote, to oppose political leaders, and to oust a serving president. But when we want to take stock of the vast changes in values, what gives people a sense of worth and membership, what people desire and fantasize about, what the role of morality is, or how clear to ourselves our identity is, things get muddled. It is difficult not only to know what to focus on in order to understand what has changed and how we have changed, but also to establish the criteria to evaluate what constitutes moral progress or decay.

There are many cultural artifacts we could assess to chart such changes across time. One intriguing line of inquiry is to think about literary best-sellers as barometers of value and to consider the differences that separate the best-sellers of different ages as markers of change. Two books published three centuries apart illustrate what I mean: Daniel Defoe's *Robinson Crusoe*, published in London in 1719 and reprinted six times in less than four months; and E. L. James's *Fifty Shades of Grey*, an erotic romance novel that topped the *New York Times* best-seller list in 2012 and has become an uncanny worldwide success. Not only three hundred years but also an abyss of cultural differences separates these two best-sellers, pointing at what separates "us" (moderns) from "them" (premoderns).[1]

Robinson Crusoe is the eponymous novel of its single hero, a man who represents the solid values of the merchant class, oriented toward duty and work. The novel documents the religious and self-introspective awakening of a man shipwrecked on a desert island and extols the values of work and self-transformation. In no way does it focus on emotions or even social relationships; indeed, the only relationship in the novel is the friendship Robinson creates with the native Friday, a relation that is more colonial domination than a reciprocal and egalitarian bond. In fact, Robinson's relation to the world writ large is one of domination and control, over both the land and its natives (Watt [1957] 2001). The novel also contains some eighteenth-century reflections on the relationship between nature and society, and much of the book's pleasure derives from seeing Robinson take possession of nature through his prescientific understanding of the rules that govern tides, weather, and crops. The novel lacks erotic or sentimental content; or, rather, if it has any eros, it is to be found in monetary exchange, international commerce, agricultural work and production, and in a dawning self-awareness that Europe had developed as a region superior to others. It is in that sense a novel of a civilization becoming aware of itself as dominating the world, and a novel about the power of a scientific understanding of an individual still steeped in faith.

1. I could also have chosen another English-language best-seller from the period, such as Samuel Richardson's *Pamela* (1740), which is much closer in content to *Fifty Shades of Grey*, but despite its success *Pamela* was widely criticized for its licentious character and is thus less suitable for this comparative exercise.

Fifty Shades of Grey takes us to far normative shores. The first volume of what became a trilogy is set on the West Coast of the New World, in Seattle, and is told from the point of view of a young adult woman, a college student named Anastasia Steele (Ana), who is still a virgin and who meets a very attractive, rich, and successful young man, Christian Grey. For the first time in her life, Ana experiences intense sexual desire, and she finds in Christian an unusual and exceptional sexual partner. Indeed, something sets Christian very far apart from other men: he will enter in a full relationship with Ana only if she signs a contract in which she willingly agrees to become his "submissive"—that is, if she agrees to be beaten, spanked, and tied, to lower her eyes in his presence, to sleep the number of hours he prescribes, and to eat only the foods and wear only the clothes he chooses for her. In addition to this contract, Ana is asked to sign a nondisclosure agreement that prevents her from divulging to anyone the nature of their relationship.

This book, then, takes us continents away from *Robinson Crusoe*. It focuses almost exclusively on love, intimacy, and sex. It is about the conquest not of land but of sentiments, the danger not of foreign and deserted landscapes but of intimate relationships, and not the self-awareness of Europe but the coming of age of a young college girl. This self-discovery is not of a spiritual nature; rather, it is of an entirely sexual and interpersonal kind. Far from endorsing conventional bourgeois morality, *Fifty Shades of Grey* presents the mainstreaming of underground sexual practices: bondage, discipline, sadism, masochism (BDSM). The relation of domination that is at the center of the book is endlessly reflected upon and negotiated, and ultimately is replaced by a relationship of love. Finally, while *Robinson Crusoe* was about learning to accept parental authority, *Fifty Shades of Grey* is about the real and symbolic scars left by bad parents, as Christian, the hero of the novel, turns out to have had a traumatized childhood, a secret the reader will only progressively discover. More generally, if *Robinson Crusoe* represents the triumph of a male-centered, Eurocentric view of morality based on values of work and self-reliance, *Fifty Shades of Grey* represents the ultimate triumph of a female point of view in culture, preoccupied with love and sexuality, with emotions, with the possibility (or impossibility) of forming enduring loving bonds with a man, and with the intertwining of pain and pleasure in romantic and sexual relationships.

To stress even further the differences in value that separate the two novels, we need only remember that one hundred years ago another novel, one that allegedly helped to spark a civil war and was full of compassion for the plight of African slaves, was dismissed at the time for being "sentimental." Today we would have no problem seeing Harriet Beecher Stowe's *Uncle Tom's Cabin* (1852) as a politically and morally ambitious novel, despite its now jarring stereotypes of people of color. But in its day, many thought the novel belonged to that dangerously feminine side of culture that would tempt readers to lapse from strict adherence to religious and moral principles and to embrace a nascent mass culture oriented toward indulgence and self-absorption (Tompkins 1986). Critics of the sentimental novel were especially worried about its emotive force: "Its dramatic power will have no other effect upon the country than to excite the fanaticism of one portion and to arouse the indignation of the other" (Pringle 1853, 7). In other words, the use of sentiment even for high moral and political purposes was low and corrupting.

Or we could take an example closer to *Fifty Shades*, Kate Chopin's now classic and canonical 1899 book *The Awakening*, a story of a married woman who discovers sexual desire and passion for another man. At the time of publication the book was greeted with general moral disgust, with one reviewer going as far as to describe its moral core as the "ugly, cruel, loathsome monster Passion," which "like a tiger ... slowly stretches its graceful length ... and ... awakens." The *New Orleans Times-Democrat* (1899) saw "unhappy Edna's awakening" as "a passion which experience has taught her is, by its very nature, evanescent" and which is "confined entirely to the senses, while reason, judgment, and all the higher faculties and perceptions ... fell into slumber deep as that of the seven sleepers" (quoted in Corse and Westervelt 2002, 139–61). The book was so coldly received by critics and readers that the discouraged Chopin turned thereafter to short stories. One cannot fail to note the contrast with E. L. James, who was instantly signed up with sequels.

In short: that a soft pornographic novel dealing with the intense absorption of two individuals in sadomasochistic sexuality could become such a worldwide best-seller a mere one hundred years after *The Awakening* gives us a glimpse at the immense change in values that must have occurred in Western culture—as dramatic a change, one might say, as electricity and indoor plumbing. Despite the danger of tautology here, I would like to suggest that best-sellers are defined by their capacity to capture values and outlooks that are either dominant and widely institutionalized or widespread enough to become mainstreamed by a cultural medium.

Best-Seller: A Definition

The 2011 erotic novel *Fifty Shades of Grey* was written by a compatriot of J. K. Rowling under the pseudonym E. L. James. Like its famous children's literature counterpart, *Fifty Shades* topped best-seller lists around the world, including lists in the

United Kingdom and even the *New York Times* in the United States. It is the first installment in a trilogy that overall has sold around forty million copies worldwide (Siegel 2012), with 32 million copies sold in the United States at the time of the writing of this essay (more than ten million copies were sold in the United States in a period of six weeks), putting the books among some of the best-selling series in all of modern publishing. Translation rights to the trilogy have been sold in thirty-seven countries, and the first volume set the record as the fastest-selling paperback of all time, surpassing even the Harry Potter series.

Best-sellers are a result of a process that started in Europe in the sixteenth century, which we may call the commodification of the book (Davis 1975). With the diminishing cost of books and rising levels of literacy, books started circulating in regional, national, and even Europe-wide markets (Eisenstein [1983] 2012). To circulate in a market means that books are bought as commodities by members of an anonymous public (as opposed to being produced for a patron, for subscribers, or for a well-known small audience of connoisseurs; or being borrowed from libraries; or being read out loud by one person for a group of listeners; etc.). The reader-consumer was thus situated at the meeting point between two overlapping but distinct spheres: he or she became a consumer located in a market, facing a range of cultural products competing with one another; and he or she (in fact, only *he* for a long time) was a citizen or member of civil society located in the sphere of public opinion.

Public opinion is the process by which ideas relevant to public and political matters are formed through interpersonal mechanisms—for example, in salons or coffee houses in the eighteenth century (Habermas 1991)—or through opinions that are more authoritative, institutionalized, public, and commodified than others (e.g., the London *Times Literary Supplement* or the *New York Times Book Review*). Some books were meant to be circulated in the private sphere (e.g., romance novels), others in the public sphere (e.g., political pamphlets), but a number of them were at the interface of the private and public divide. Pornographic or erotic literature, for example, was located at the interface of the two, as it circulated in the private sphere (and was read mostly by the upper classes) but had deep political implications in challenging the power of the church (Hunt 1991). Interestingly enough, as censorship and the church lost power, pornographic and erotic literature, while it remained highly controlled and regulated, lost its political power, becoming an object of private consumption. The advent of the Internet further commodified pornography for private consumption.

In the relatively short history of the commodification of the book, a crucial development occurred after World War II. With the consolidation of many large corporate publishing industries in the 1940s, the attempt to control the elements conducive to a best-seller grew (Schiffrin 2001). The war proved a benefit to the book business, with rapid sales of books relevant to the war leading to increased sales in other genres. This period marked the first time that publishers began operating as real businesses, as they took their first cues from the marketplace about how to tailor books to specific readers (ibid., 148). Especially after the end of the Cold War, a new ideology that emphasized belief in the market and its values took hold. This belief, that the market represented a consumer democracy, became the hallmark of publishing and led to the trend of smaller publishers increasingly merging into international conglomerates. The editors in these conglomerates encouraged a concentration on a handful of books that would allow them to meet the economic expectations of corporate owners (ibid., 150). And suburbanization further contributed to the commodification of the book in changing the nature of the bookstore: "The only way for suburban booksellers to thrive—as well as chain bookstores—was to reduce the shelf space dedicated to slow-moving inventory and devote more space to the best-sellers" (ibid., 151).

The importance of best-sellers was the natural outcome of the commodification of publishing and its emphasis on marketing. Indeed, although the literary world uses an antimarketing rhetoric (Brown 2011,76), the book trade was driven by marketing practices from the Renaissance through the twentieth century. Some examples include William Caxton's anticipation of straight-through processing principles between 1476 and 1492, Mason Locke Weems's Bible in the early nineteenth century, and the exploitation of Tarzan in the 1920s and 30s.[2] In addition, many known writers worked in areas related to marketing, such as advertisement and business, before their success (ibid., 73–74). (By the way, E. L. James herself, the author of *Fifty Shades of Grey*, was a television executive, a position that would have made her familiar with the question of how to fit a cultural product to a public.)

Another example of a best-seller series that was created based on marketing practices can be seen in the case of the writer James L. Patterson. Patterson, a former advertiser by trade, made the first book in the Alex Cross series a best-seller by exploiting his experience. He created and published the book in a manner "that owes more to Dunkin Donuts than Doubleday, more to KFC than Knopf" (Brown 2011, 75). Unhappy with his publisher's poor marketing efforts, Patterson

2. As Stephen Brown succinctly puts it, "Literary types are neither commercially naive nor as unwilling to sell themselves as they are sometimes made out to be" (2011, 70–86; see esp. 70–76).

replaced the cover and funded a television advertisement campaign. The book quickly became a best-seller, and thereby Patterson established the fast-fiction formula.[3] Between 1976 and 2011, Patterson published seventy-three thrills-and-spills-filled titles that sold approximately 200 million worldwide. His novels come in clearly defined ranges, and the production was outsourced to teams of coauthors, which allowed Patterson to produce five or six books per year (ibid., 75).

Best-seller lists are increasingly populated by authors produced in a system where the market and marketing techniques prevail (Verboord 2011, 290–315). Competition between book titles and authors has intensified considerably, but authors who write genre fiction and series or who have "star power" seem to thrive better (ibid., 308); authors who have established a large literary status appear less often in the lists and have shorter stays; and what is classified as a best-seller diverges more and more from what critics classify as aesthetically important work (ibid., 308–9). The divergence between the economic and cultural fields, in other words, is itself an effect of an intense commodification of the latter field.

When a book becomes a best-seller, it means very simply that it is in the category that sells most. BookScan US, a division of the famous ratings agency Nielsen, is perhaps the most aggressive attempt to produce a completely automatic and trusted set of best-seller lists. BookScan gathers data directly from sales to customers by Amazon and other Internet sellers and at more than forty-five hundred retail locations—including a variety of retailers: many independent bookstores, large chains such as Barnes & Noble, Powell's Books, (formerly) Borders, and the general retailer Costco (Gross 2006;

3. Brown (2011, 75) describes this formula as consisting of very short chapters, nonstop action, all plot, and no palaver.

Longhofer, Golden, and Baiocchi 2010, 18–25). The *New York Times*'s way of compiling its own best-selling list is a notoriously well-kept secret, and one can only surmise that it similarly combines sales data at cash registers and in book orders. While best-sellers feature a variety of topics,[4] romance novels represent the prime commodification of the book, as they are produced by large worldwide corporations. The Harlequin series, for example, uses extensive marketing research to calibrate its formulas to the changing tastes of its readers (Regis 2011; Thurston 1987). Harlequin Corporation publishes romances and women's literature with few competitors worldwide: each month it publishes 110 titles that are translated and distributed in thirty-one countries. Romance novels

---

4. To the question of what makes a best-seller, scholars found that definite themes sold better: sensationalism, themes of religion, and adventure recur frequently in best-sellers. E. Haldeman-Julius (1928, 138–78) found that many of his books sold much better when given new titles that contain themes of love, sex, religion, self-improvement, and humor. Similarly, G. Hicks (1934, 621–29) concluded that the recommended novel formula should include "a lively story, largely romantic in theme and setting with conventional characters and plot and some pretention to a message or thesis, apparently profound but really commonplace." E. Weeks (1936:2–15) studied Margaret Mitchell's *Gone with the Wind* (1939) and deduced that the following factors in the proportions indicated were responsible for its success: timelessness (45%), emotion (25%), characterization (15%), invention (10%), and advertising (5%). Furthermore, in a study by J. Harvey, "emotion" was found to be a major ingredient of the best-seller (1953, 91–114]); certain characteristics of the central male character are either positively or negatively associated with sales (109); and there are certain stylistic and thematic differences between best and poor sellers (108). The most important factors associated with sales are emotion, the personalities of the major characters, the plot themes, and simplicity (ibid., 110).

are one of the most commodified sectors of the book industry, if not its most commodified, in the sense that books are produced according to very well researched and standardized formulas. Romances are also one of the most profitable sectors of the publishing industry, worth more than a billion dollars a year, according to the website of Romance Writers of America (RWA). Romance novels constitute 46 percent of all mass market paperbacks sold in the United States, and according to Harlequin, over half its customers buy an average of 30 novels a month" (Linden and Rees 1992, 70–75). The RWA's website indicates that "romance fiction revenue actually increased from $1.355 billion in 2010 to $1.368 billion in 2011, and it remains the largest share of the consumer market at 14.3 percent." And more than seventy-four million people claimed to have read at least one romance novel in 2008, according to an RWA study posted on its site. Nine percent of romance readers identified themselves as male, and the study reported that the majority of romance readers were married or living with a partner. According to Harlequin, in the "About Us" section on its site, the company sells more than four books per second, half of them internationally. In the UK, over 20 percent of all fiction books sold each year are romance novels.

Few genres are more clearly gendered than the romance novel. The numbers reveal a genre that has perfected the art of offering to its (mostly) female readers what nourishes their fantasies. Given that *Fifty Shades of Grey* mixes the genres of traditional and erotic romance novel, one wonders how it distinguished itself in the already flourishing book industry to stand above other books and series. Precisely because nowadays formal attempts to shape opinion precede informal ones (e.g., with marketing campaigns, endorsements, prepublication of excerpts in large-circulation magazines, etc.), we must ask ourselves why *Fifty Shades of Grey* provides a spectacular example of the opposite process—that is, a relatively informal diffusion that occurred before formal mainstream sales.

The Power of Cultural Resonance

Trying to understand what makes a book into a best-seller starts with a certain amount of bad faith. Most of the time no one predicts a book's success, and yet once it succeeds, it looks as if this success was inevitable. In that sense, it seems as if we are trying to find compelling reasons for something we could not have predicted in the first place. This bad faith is even more blatant in the case of cultural artifacts like *Fifty Shades* that seem to contravene established norms (they only seem to, however, because sadomasochism has been a part of the literary canon since at least the writings of the Marquis de Sade, and because a large number of Harlequin novels had been mainstreaming eroticism for the past two decades).

But we can evade this conundrum if we agree that explaining the reasons for a best-seller is not the same as predicting its success. A software program or algorithm may be able to predict the success of a book or blockbuster, yet it is doubtful whether the software can explain its own success. Explaining requires us to understand the relationship between the mechanisms of diffusion of a text (marketing, Internet), the text itself (its genres and conventions), and the ways in which it resonates with the experience of people who read it and the meanings they attribute to it.

In his own best-selling study of successful brands, *The Tipping Point* ([2000] 2003), Malcolm Gladwell has made the sociological point that the success of fads and fashions derives from three principal factors: they are transmitted through people located in the right places (in his flashy terminology: Mavens, Connectors, and Salesmen); these new ideas or objects have some "stickiness" (they are presented in a convincing way); and they appear in the right context. Underestimating the sociological underpinnings of his own theory, Gladwell suggests that new ideas spread like microbes and epidemics—that is, by contagion, or as Richard Dawkins ([1976] 2006) puts it, through memes. This theory—which views key actors as central to the process of spreading an idea or product—explains how new consumer objects or key cultural concepts spread in domains of culture in which formal agencies and gatekeeping mechanisms play key roles. The theory is less well suited, however, to explaining the spread of ideas or books that use well-trodden formulas, such as *Fifty Shades of Grey*, and that initially largely spread through word of mouth rather than through formal marketing agencies. *Fifty Shades* spread informally, and its combination of conventional narrative formula and BDSM were probable catalysts for its rapid spread. Yet the question remains: why this particular story?

In an oft-quoted article, Michael Schudson (1989, 153–80) tries to understand why some ideas and texts become widely visible and spread more rapidly than others. Schudson gives the following example:

From 1944 to 1946, George Kennan had been sending memos from the American Embassy in Moscow that, he recalls, "made no impression whatsoever in Washington, if, indeed, they were ever read." In 1946, with wartime cooperation over, with Ambassador Harriman returning home and Kennan in charge, the State Department asked him for an opinion on how to explain Soviet behavior. Kennan took a hard-line stance as he had for several years, arguing that the Soviet leaders were stubborn autocrats who could not be trusted. The reaction in Washington, Kennan writes in his memoirs, was "nothing less than sensational": It was one of those moments when official Washington, whose states of receptivity are intricately imbedded in the subconscious, was ready to receive a given message.... Six months earlier it would have been received in the Department of State with raised eyebrows and lips pursed in disapproval. Six months later, it would probably have sounded redundant, a sort of preaching to the convinced.... Then what did the memo do? It is not easy to say. It would be too much to say that it was the decisive factor in changing American policy toward the Soviet Union. Did it accelerate a shift in policy? Or crystallize a shift already underway? Cultural analysis requires a language for action like this, poised somewhere between determination and ineffectuality. (159)

Schudson defines the problem here very well. A report that six months earlier would have been ignored or dismissed became "sensational," suggesting that the success of a text has to do with its conditions of reception; that is, with the values, ideas, expectations, representations, and images that people develop prior to encountering the text, and that these conditions can sometimes change rapidly. This is related to the approach that anthropologist Dan Sperber calls an "epidemiology of representations," which answers the question "why are some representations more 'catching' than others?" (quoted in ibid., 158). The answer to this question must address what a text is made to mean in a certain context, and what impact this meaning has on the context itself.

Schudson identifies five main factors to explain the success of an idea. One is *retrievablility*: "if a cultural object is to reach people, it must be 'available' to them" (161). The second is *rhetorical force*: "there is something, even if that something is far from being everything, to a concept of art or craft, something to the idea that one person or group may create a cultural object more vivid, funny, appealing, graphic, dramatic, suspenseful, interesting, beautiful, stunning than another" (166). The third factor is *resonance*, or the relevance of a cultural object to its audience. As Schudson puts it, the utility of the text is a property not only of the object's content or nature and the audience's interest in it, but also of the position of the object in the cultural tradition of the society the audience is a part of. Against an individualistic view of needs, Schudson suggests that clearly "the needs or interests of an audience are socially and culturally constituted" (169). The next criterion is *institutional retention*, by which he means that an idea or story must be institutionalized. A cultural object "becomes a part of common reference" for its power to reach wide and large (170). The last criterion Schudson calls *resolution*. "Some elements in culture," he writes, "are more likely to influence action than others because they are better situated at a point of action or because they are by nature directives for action. An advertisement is a cultural text of high 'resolution' in that it normally tells the audience precisely what to do to respond. It says: go out and buy" (171).

Retrievability, rhetorical force, resonance, retention, and resolution thus form the five *R*s, explaining how ideas embodied in objects and institutions spread quickly, and they already indicate the reasons for the success of *Fifty Shades of Grey*: its high retrievability through the Internet and e-reading devices; its rhetorical force contained in its pornographic/erotic content; and its resonance with a culture in which sexuality has increasingly become autonomized, an independent field of action containing its own rules and moral values. The institutional retention of the book is to be found in the fact that it mobilized so many social organizations: Internet sites, the publishing industry, the movie industry, the sex toys industry, booksellers, women's discussion groups, a wide variety of media programs, and feminist groups. Finally, its "resolution" consists in the fact that the book has presumably had a significant impact on the sexual lives of its readers, increasing the purchase of sex toys and a wide variety of spinoff consumer items.

But given the prior wide availability of pornography on the Internet and in public culture more generally, the sexual content cannot possibly be the *only* explanation for this novel's success (Douglas 1980, 25–29). What the "mommy porn" argument cannot explain is the fact that readers became so passionately involved with this specific story and engaged in extensive conversations about it, this when so much soft-core porn was already available and when Harlequin itself had long been offering erotic romance novels. Moreover, while Schudson's and Gladwell's models are useful, they do not differentiate between advertising messages that promote a particular product, a consumer brand, a news item, and a romance novel. Surely there must be differences among them. Advertising and news are mostly about attention grabbing and involve the reader's self only minimally. Literary forms, on the other hand, involve complex and extended processes of identification with characters, rehearsals of possible developments and likely ends, a reflection on the moral meaning of characters' choices, and inferences about the causality of characters' behavior. Explaining the success of complex narrative structures requires elements present in the success of a brand (such as rhetorical force) but differs from it as well in entailing a far more complex process of cultural resonance because it contains various characters, takes different points of view, and plots a story that encodes social experience in a nonstraightforward way.

To put this more precisely: when trying to understand the success of a best-seller, we must distinguish between at least two phases: one, in which the book initially takes off and reaches the magic threshold; and the other, in which the object becomes publicly *known* as a "best-seller," in which case its attraction becomes intertwined with its fashionableness, the fact that people want to read simply for that reason. In other words, the first group of highly motivated people do not appropriate the book in the same way or for the same reasons as those who buy the book after it is well known and publicized as a best-seller. Those in the first group are motivated by emotional and aesthetic reasons, that is, by the desire to appropriate a story line and formula whose rules they are usually familiar with; the second group is motivated by a consumer dynamic of imitation and distinction, wanting to know what others know. Gladwell and Schudson do not distinguish enough between the two groups and are oblivious to the power of the story itself in helping shape the first group of avid, devoted, and committed consumers. That stories and other cultural materials have an intrinsic power that needs to be explained is the core assumption of the study of texts.

One of the most remarkable features of *Fifty Shades of Grey* is that its initial success happened under the radar of corporations and relied almost exclusively on a highly committed group of readers who interacted in the public sphere of the Internet, a public sphere that blurs in an unprecedented way the private and the public, the noncommercial and the commercial. This could happen because James (then still named Leonard) wrote an earlier version of this book as fan fiction in a popular FanFiction forum on the Internet.

Fan fiction is interactive narrative, usually loosely connected to popular books, TV shows, and movies, written by nonprofessionals and professionals, and to which the audience responds. In Leonard/James's case, the fans for whom she wrote are followers of the popular vampire-themed *Twilight* novels and movies. Like many fan fiction writers, Leonard/James uploaded her work *Master of the Universe* in serial installments, a method that enables readers to respond as the story progresses and that also allows writers to incorporate the readers' feedback as they write and develop the story. Many contemporary popular books and TV programs are indeed characterized by a blurring of the process of production and the process of reception, making the two virtually inseparable, or rather, making reception a part of the writing/production process, thus communicating directly with readers' and viewers' fantasies. This process is called "prosumption," and it is one of the most significant transformations of the process of consumption, allowing the consumer-viewer-reader in some sense to create the commodity she or he is consuming. In its fan fiction Internet version, *Fifty Shades of Grey* (like the *Oprah Winfrey Show* or reality TV) directly incorporated suggestions by readers, so that we can presume that the meanings and plot twists that readers wanted to find were incorporated into the narrative. Further, writers can infer from the number and tenor of readers' responses which fan fiction stories are most popular. In other words, these sites have built-in mechanisms for marketing and audience research. The writer can incorporate readers' wishes and desires as the writing goes along. In that sense the text can be said to reflect straightforwardly the audience's fantasies, even the contradictory character of these fantasies (Parks 2012). The narrative elements of this story, then, are intricately intertwined in the novel's origin as a prosumption commodity—that is, a commodity in which the consumer does much of the work previously done by producers (e.g., cleaning food or assembling furniture).

Some comments concerning the sexual nature of the material compelled James eventually to remove the story from websites and to publish it on her own. Before the novel's publication in print form, James removed the material from her own website. The first volume, titled *Fifty Shades of Grey*, was released as an e-book and a print-on-demand paperback in May 2011 by a virtual publisher based in Australia. This virtual publisher relied largely on book blogs for early publicity, and sales of the novel were boosted by word-of-mouth recommendation. By January 2012, when the final volume was released, the *Fifty Shades* trilogy was an example of highly successful viral marketing.

In this essay I do not claim to explain and understand the many ways in which the text of *Fifty Shades* incorporated readers' comments (this information is not available), nor do I attempt to document the different interpretations of the narrative. Rather, I would like to understand how the intense reading pleasure it created resonates with the sociological structure of men and women's relationships today.

Resonate is here an advisedly vague word, for if it is not always easy to understand *why* a book becomes a best-seller, we can say with a modicum of certainty that the narratives contained *in* best-sellers cannot be foreign to the collective preoccupations of a culture, its values, anxieties, and fantasies. Literature—good or bad—puts into form what is often at the level of inarticulate social experience, what Raymond Williams (1975) called a structure of feeling. To the sociologist of culture, best-sellers are nothing but proxies to take stock of the mechanisms that bring a book to best-selling status and of the cultural climate that makes a story—its characters, plot, resolution—relevant to an epoch. In this sense, my analysis of this best-seller consists in nothing more than offering a plausible interpretation of its *fit* to the cultural structures of late capitalist and postfeminist countries. The fogginess of the notion of "resonance" is thus necessary, as it captures the dense and invisible threads that connect a particular story to the personal lives and social experience of its readers. Understanding a story is not simply a cognitive process but a diffuse and complex process of using culture (its values, stories, ideals) to make sense of one's social experience. However vague, then, the guiding assumption of this essay is that we cannot fully capture the range of causes that turn a book into a best-seller. We can, however, try to understand how it articulates the core cultural values and key experiences of the society in which it circulates. This, indeed, is what this book is about. Such exercise is not an explanation but an attempt to understand why some narratives are so "fitting" to their society.

The "resonance" of a novel with its society operates at a number of levels. The most obvious is that a book repeats and prolongs a well-known set of questions and uses conventional forms and values to address them. Resonance in that sense means the use and recognition of the familiar, as when advertising for lipstick or detergent resonates with established gender roles (e.g., women are preoccupied with the color of their lips, or women clean the house). But a book can also resonate when it formulates something that many people *want* to say but are unable to say, either because they do not dare say it (e.g., that women still fantasize about powerful and domineering men) or because they do not have the language to say it (e.g., that the state of modern sexuality produces anxieties and difficulties that have not been adequately theorized, and that have thus remained without a name or a language). A book resonates when it articulates—sometimes directly and sometimes in a roundabout way—a social experience that is baffling, that presents itself as a repeated cognitive and emotional challenge. For example, John Gray's *Men Are from Mars, Women Are from Venus* ([1992] 2004) became a worldwide best-seller because it addressed and (seemingly) "explained" the misunderstandings and tangible differences between the sexes with crisp metaphors (Mars and Venus). It resonated with the fact that men and women are both equal and profoundly different, behaving differently in relationships. *Resonate* here means that a narrative is able not only to address a social experience that is not adequately understood, named, or categorized but also to "frame" it in an adequate explanatory way. Finally, *resonate* can also mean that a book offers recipes and guidelines that can be incorporated into people's lives. Ellen Fein and Sherrie Schneider's worldwide best-selling series *The Rules* ([1995] 2007), for example, provided guidelines to women on how to "catch" elusive men by limiting their own availability and restricting how much interest they show in the men.

If one of the insights of deconstruction is that literature is the performance of a problem, that a literary text enacts the contours of a contradiction, an impossibility, or the unresolvable character of a situation, we may generalize this claim to texts that resonate with readers and suggest that such resonance is explained broadly by the fact that the text performs a problem. Further, we may add that in contradistinction to high culture, popular texts not only enact a problem but resolve it as well.[5]

My claim is that the narrative of *Fifty Shades* stages many of the aporias of the sexual relationships between men and women and that the sadomasochistic relationship depicted in *Fifty Shades* is both a symbolic solution for and a practi-

5. Eyal Peretz has inspired and illuminated me in this regard.

cal technique to overcome these aporias. What, then, makes a story able to resonate so closely with the preoccupations of a culture? I explore this question next.

Popular Stories as Codes for Social Experience[6]

In his study of traditional folktales, Robert Darnton (2009) has shown that the tales consistently addressed the "difficult social and economic conditions" of peasant life in premodern Europe. The plots and narrative structures of these folktales could be readily explained by the demography and economy of premodern Europe: the frequent appearance of stepparents can be interpreted as emanating from the high proportion of remarriages due to spouses' deaths; the frequent theme of magic tables filling with delicious food can be explained by the pervasiveness of hunger and famines; and the prevalence of tricksters reflects the fact that commoners often evaded and manipulated feudal regulations. In short, Darnton suggests that the social and physical environment of premodern European peasants is both the background and the content of these folktales and that, far from expressing universal psychic structures, these folktales incorporated and mirrored specific social and economic conditions of the peasants who listened to and told them. Darnton speculates that these tales served as *cognitive maps* to help peasants make sense of the harsh and arbitrary conditions of their lives.

In a similar vein, best-sellers are likely to be texts that encode problematic social conditions—that is, social conditions that threaten individuals' capacity to pursue certain central goals be they satiety, happiness, or material wealth. A prob-

6. This section until p. 26 is adapted from my 2003 book *Oprah Winfrey and the Glamour of Misery*.

lematic social condition is a situation in which there is an incongruence between the ordinary goals people want to reach and the resources that are available to them. Indeed modern polities are saturated with contradictions (between social spheres, norms, roles, and values) and rife with the moral dilemmas that follow from them.

Endemic contradictions and dilemmas produce a sense of disorientation for the self. It follows from this that popular texts are likely to be precisely those texts that encode and address *social contradictions*, and that those cultural enterpreneurs who, for biographical and structural reasons, stand at the meeting point of contradictions that are central to modern polities are likely to produce powerful symbolic forms. Oprah Winfrey is a good example of such an entrepreneur. Benjamin Spock's and T. Berry Brazelton's famous books on child rearing are additional examples. Sharon Hays (1996) has suggested that these books succeeded because they addressed women in their dual and contradictory roles as experts and traditional caregivers—positions previously experienced as mutually exclusive. Moreover, these books demand from women that they apply to child rearing simultaneously a romantic ethic of unconditional love and a rational form of nurturance based on scientific-therapeutic views. In short, institutionalized contradictions can produce disorientation, and texts that encode these contradictions can become popular, especially those that provide a sense of guidance to help the self reorient itself.

My second hypothesis immediately follows: texts are likely to be popular when they offer (symbolic) resolutions to social contradictions. These symbolic contradictions can find a resolution in certain characters who mix incompatible attributes (e.g., the trickster is both weak and strong), or in the form of particular narrative closure (in *Romeo and Juliet*, for instance, the death of lovers reconciles both the affirmation of love against family and the requirements of a society that cannot allow love as a basis for marriage).

Precisely because popular texts often address social contradictions, they are also likely to provide a sense of guidance in a difficult and chaotic social order. Folktales, child-rearing books, and romance novels provide a sense of direction for the self in the midst of painful conditions and social contradictions. Popular culture, then, provides a sense of direction; it says clearly and unambiguously: *this is how things should be done.* But in modern societies, such sense-making and guidance is assumed by the rapidly proliferating self-help culture, including psychological, medical, and spiritual guidance in a wide variety of domains. This culture has in turn spilled over into many other domains, turning into what we may call a generalized self-help cultural mode. The self-help genre may have had its origins in Stoic philosophy, geared at helping to control one's emotions through mental exercises. But it rose to generalized prominence and commercial success in the nineteenth century (note, for example, the success of the 1845 *Self-Help* written by Samuel Smiles). The explicit purpose of such guides, written by the clergy, laymen, and laywomen with moral authority, on a variety of subjects such as work, upward mobility, education, and marriage, was to shape and orient the self in a society whose norms were becoming increasingly elusive and complex. When individuals became socially and geographically mobile, that is, individualized, (new) social rules and strategies were needed to help shape individual goals.

With the advent of clinical psychology and Freudianism, self-help culture took a far deeper hold on American culture and became a dominant way for the individual to relate to his or her self, viewing his or her emotional makeup as *in need* of shaping. This self-help cultural mode has also spilled over into mass media in general (talk shows, for example) and has become a fundamental way to organize modern subjectivity. Where individuals used to shape their behavior by relying on dos and don'ts inscribed in communities, they now shape their behavior from the center of the self, so to speak, through conscious acts of volition, by explicitly stating goals, and by using the expert knowledge of a psychologist, doctor, media figure, or spiritual guru. Such a self-help cultural mode is present in the narrative of *Fifty Shades of Grey*, which, while not advertised as being in this genre, does offer techniques and recipes that may be directly incorporated into one's sexual life. However, while the self-help mode is usually proffered within a rhetoric of what is realistically feasible, in *Fifty Shades* the self-help is actually contained in and issued through an erotic fantasy. The story in which the fantasy is told is about the sexual encounter of two sexualized bodies and should be interpreted in the broader context of what Lauren Berlant (1995, 379–404) calls "the transformation of the body in mass national society and thinking about a structure of political feeling that characterizes the history of national sentimentality." That body, presented as a simultaneous site of pleasure and pain, is in fact the main protagonist of this story. It is this body that activates the fantasy of the reader.

In its psychoanalytical meaning, *fantasy* refers to a thought process that is disconnected from reality; either it is a distorted memory from an actual event that took place, or it is that which hides from the self the reality of its instincts (Laplanche and Pontalis 1974). In *The Interpretation of Dreams*, Sigmund Freud offers an additional perspective and views fantasy in terms that are very similar to dreams: that is, as *compromise formations*. In a compromise formation, the subject is unable to directly express her or his wishes—they must remain unconscious—and develops "symptoms" that at once express and deny the wish. The neurosis, fantasy, and dream then have the same function: they contain that which they deny and oppose; they thus address obliquely and indirectly a desire; they say without saying; they simultaneously contain and deny a certain reality. Dreams, fantasies, and neuroses address the world in this way because consciousness is obliged to repress content. Repressed content can refer to a taboo (sociologically: something deemed illegitimate) or to an object that elicits pain (e.g., desiring someone who regularly hurts and abandons us). Fantasy is not only a way to transcend the limitations of reality but also a way to incorporate that reality into the very gesture of fleeing from it (e.g., I may fantasize about hurting the person I actually desire).

What is so powerful, then, about the Freudian notion is its view that fantasy both presents and distorts reality. Fantasy works around reality, incorporates it, defends the self *against* reality, and yet helps one live *with* it. In this view, a fantasy is a mediation between different systems, it includes that which it denies, and it offers a transition between different aspects of consciousness. We may surmise that this is also the reason that fantasy plays a crucial role in psychic and collective life, precisely because it addresses conflicts and deprivations and helps resolve them.

To say that popular fiction generates fantasy is thus to say that it simultaneously expresses and evades a component of one's social and collective reality. Self-help culture, on the other hand, bridges the text and the real by providing recipes, ways of doing things. My claim here is that a large extent of women's culture is a variation of self-help culture, a toolkit to guide the self (via women's magazines, self-help manuals, romance novels, talk shows), sometimes using therapeutic or spiritual guidance, or by making fantasy follow the prescriptive mode of self-help (see Norwood 2008; Shipside 2008; Tegarden 2004; Thoele 2001).

Such a mode of appropriation of texts by women makes intensive use of what literary scholar Louise Rosenblatt (1987) has identified as "efferent transactions," that is, "readings that are motivated mainly by a search for something to 'carry away.'" Some readers will read even fiction of the least didactic kind "efferently," that is, in the search for some practical guidance or some special wisdom, or for what Wayne Booth has called some useful "carry-over" into nonfictional life (Booth 1988). Women's popular literature articulates pleasure as a useful carryover of fantasy in their daily lives. Fantasy is pleasurable because it erases privation and conflict simply by declaring them not to exist (among hungry European peasants, claiming that in paradise tables are always filled with delicious food; in science fiction, making humans able to fly and read each other's minds).

Another, perhaps even more effective, way to produce pleasure is to bind and overcome opposites by showing a heroine to be both feminine and able to act as a killer (see, for example, the blockbuster films *La Femme Nikita* and later *Kill Bill*, whose pleasure had to do with the fact that the heroines' bodies had the fragility of femininity and the self-controlled power of aggressive masculinity.) Here fantasy works by its capacity to enact and transcend tensions, that is, by making A and not-A simultaneously possible. But self-help produces pleasure because it is located at the seamless interface of reality and fantasy; it provides instructions—explicit or hidden—to improve one's life and overcome conflicts and dilemmas, thus making reading performative (that is, the enactment of what it talks about), and making that very performativity pleasurable by translating fantasy into reality. Indeed, as Lauren Berlant put it in her *The Female Complaint* (2008), the modern women's culture that has been forged within and by the market is about the belief that emotion can change reality. It is this central belief that forms the core of self-help culture. The fantasy that the self-help cultural mode enacts, then, is the fantasy of a self-generated and self-shaping self. Self-help is a fantasy about the self in motion and action. The self-help cultural mode makes fictional fantasy provide the tools to control and change daily life.

My argument for the remainder of this essay is that *Fifty Shades of Grey* offers BDSM as a cultural—rather than sexual—fantasy because BDSM transcends the tensions of sexual relations and functions as a self-help category, a recipe for a better sexual and romantic life. *Fifty Shades* must then be understood as a genre that intertwines closely a commentary on the deprived condition of love and sexuality, a romantic fantasy, and self-help instructions on how to improve that life. It encodes the aporias of heterosexual relationships, offers a fantasy for overcoming these aporias, and functions as a self-help sexual manual. This threefold movement of the narrative explains, at least partly, why it became a far-reaching best-seller.

2 / How to Find Emotional Certainty in a World of Sexual Uncertainty

Fifty Shades of Grey is about a girl, Anastasia (Ana), who is finishing college and who is initiated into sex, love, and a profession (a career in publishing) through her relationship with a man who practices an exquisitely elaborate form of sadomasochistic sex. All of the volumes in the *Fifty Shades* series are written from Ana's point of view; that is, we hear her thoughts and feelings for Christian Grey. The first volume—the one most widely sold—revolves around the question of knowing who the mysterious and terrifyingly attractive man called Christian Grey is. The second volume is about Ana and Christian's discovery of each other's deep feelings and mutual commitment, ending in a marriage proposal. It is also about the discovery that the self-possessed Christian Grey's biological mother was a cocaine-addicted prostitute, that his father was violent, and that he is an adopted child of a loving and socially well-established family. The third volume is about their married life and Ana's struggles to achieve autonomy when Christian becomes the owner of the publishing company in which she works.

A Woman's Novel

This is a women's novel, written by a woman, read (mostly) by women, clearly marketed to women, and more appreciated by women than by men. As a German man living in London whose reaction I solicited through e-mail put it: "My girlfriend was fascinated by the book and told me that she believes 'every man should read this book in order to understand what women want from a man.'" With such a ringing endorsement, I flicked through a few pages of the book, then put it aside. I was speechless. It contained some of the worst writing I have ever seen and a plot that made my toenails curl. An article published on the web stresses the point aptly: "The bondage-inflected romance novel *50 Shades of Grey* has topped the *New York Times* bestseller lists for 10 weeks, followed at numbers two and three by its two sequels. It's been most popular with women, especially moms, leading many to call it (dismissively or worshipfully, depending on their point of view) 'mommy porn'" (North 2012). This opinion is shared by the readers themselves, as illustrated by the author of a book blog:

> I enjoyed *50 Shades of Grey* enough to pick up the next book in the series, but I never dreamed I'd spend 1,000 words defending it. Perhaps, I'm really defending myself and other women who read the book and didn't hate it, or actually loved it, or whatever. Because a lot of the eye-rolling at this book feels like the usual attack on women and the things women like and the usual underestimation of our ability to know our own minds. (Harris 2012)

Without a doubt, the book enacts contemporary women's fantasies.

But what exactly are "women's" fantasies? The novel treads highly familiar ground for women. Since the eighteenth century, and most definitely since the nineteenth, with the institutionalization of the private sphere and of the emotional family (defined as a unit whose vocation is to forge and maintain emotional bonds between its members), romance novels have given expression to women's search for love and matrimony in a pleasurable formula in which the heroine meets an attractive but dark and threatening man, who later reveals himself to love her and be devoted to her (Charlotte Brontë's *Jane Eyre* is a prototype, and even Samuel Richardson's bestseller *Pamela* may be viewed as an initiator of this genre). *Fifty Shades of Grey* is an almost caricatural version of a gothic romance in its use of such familiar themes: the innocent and virtuous but opinionated young woman who works for a rich man who behaves to her in a seemingly hurtful way, with the novel progressively revealing his tangled past, his vulnerability, and his uncompromised devotion to her.

The second way in which this novel is tailor-made for women is in its graphic exposition of sex within the account of a conventional heterosexual relationship geared to women who live in conventional domestic frameworks ("mommy porn"). The mommy porn genre takes place in the context of the "pornification" of culture—the mainstreaming of pornography in culture—and the growing consumption of pornography by women.[1] Undoubtedly, *Fifty Shades*'s depiction of

1. Jessica Bennett claimed in a *Daily Beast* article (2008) that "according to a 2007 study from the University of Alberta, as many as 90 percent of boys and 70 percent of girls aged 13 to 14 have accessed sexually explicit content at least once." Tanith Carey (2011) says in a *Guardian* article that "it's accepted that women are watching—and enjoying—porn more and more.... While more than six out of 10 women say they view

sex is a part of this worldwide trend. Yet the terms "mommy porn" and "pornification" ignore the complex cultural structure of women's sexuality—which serves the purposes of not only pleasure, freedom, and power but also identity projects and the management of close and intimate relationships. If the nineteenth-century novel was about the self-discovery of a young woman through love, contemporary popular texts aimed at women now ask, what is to be discovered about oneself when engaging in an active sex life, free of matrimonial goals and constraints? Sexual liberation has provided new practices for women to "reclaim" sexuality as a positive and moral aspect of their identity (see, for example, the worldwide success of Eve Ensler's *Vagina Monologues* as a direct expression of this reclaiming of women's sex and body).

Fifty Shades of Grey is unquestionably inscribed in this trend and subscribes to the unforgettable injunction issued by feminist writer Germaine Greer: "Lady, Love your Cunt." (And Naomi Wolf's recent *Vagina* seems to have followed that trail.) But such reclaiming of one's body and sexuality interacts (or comes into conflict) with another traditional thick woman's social world, made of sentiments, obligations to others, and domestic bonds. Sexual freedom, for women, is complexly entangled with the longing for intimacy, which is why it has generated a question that has reverberated in women's popular culture for the last six decades: what ought to be the value, the form, and the limits of a free sexuality? For example, the worldwide TV series and phenomenon *Sex and*

---

web porn, one study in 2006 by the Internet Filter Review found that 17% of women describe themselves as "addicted." Furthermore, Feona Attwood (2005, 65–86, 72), based on an article by Loretta Loach (1992, 266–74), claimed that "in 1992 some statistics appeared to be indicating that the numbers of female porn consumers were growing, representing 30% of the total in Australia and 40% in the United States" (270–72).

the City (and more recently the widely popular HBO *Girls*) revolves around the question of what is a "female point of view" on sexuality, whether the longing for monogamous love is or is not compatible with feminist politics (McRobbie 1991, 94). If *Fifty Shades of Grey* is a women's novel, it is precisely in the sense that, for women, sexuality is at once a site of self-knowledge and self-identity and a *problem*. More than for men, modern women's sexuality has been caught in the tensions between sexual freedom and the traditional social structure of the family, between the desire for individual pleasure and the injunction to fulfill the duties of a domestic unit. This is in turn the reason why *Fifty Shades of Grey* cannot be characterized as being simply and only mommy porn—unless one naively assumes that the romance is the "pretext" to wrap the sex in the pink paper of sentiments. In fact, the opposite is the case: it is the sex that is the pink paper in which the love story is wrapped. For in the new culture of sexual autonomy, it is the fantasy of and for total love that has become unavowable. In an April 2013 interview in the French magazine *Le Point*, the famous French writer Michel Houellebecq commented on the notion that love had become unavowable. He was asked by the journalist if he still believed in love. Houellebecq replied:

MH: People believe in it. And I believe in it too.... In fact, people believe in it today much more than during my childhood.
LP: Why?
MH: I don't know. We can try to understand. We can say they don't believe in politics anymore, or in brotherhood. That they pretend they believe in friendship, without fooling themselves entirely. So they still form couples, or at least try to. They think it is sad to live alone. Then there is this aggressive attitude against love, you know, like during the 1970s.

The stupid idea according to which sentimentality is more pornographic than pornography. I was never shocked either by pornography or by sentimentality.

Houellebecq suggests that the portrayal and experience of love are now in crisis: people have sentimental longings they cannot acknowledge anymore, and this is because, I would argue, heteronormativity—the norms regulating men and women's relationships—has itself run into a crisis. As Lauren Berlant (1995) claims: "At moments of crisis, persons violate the zones of privacy that give them privilege and protection in order to fix something social that feels threatening: they practice politics, they generate publicity, they act in public, but in the name of privacy." *Fifty Shades of Grey* gives publicity to what has become a crisis of sexual privacy.

For the nonsociologist, sex is the sinful or the pleasurable act we do in the privacy of our bedroom. For the sociologist, sex and sexuality are an axis around which the social order is organized, an axis that binds or divides people in specific and predictable patterns. Whom one is allowed or prohibited to have sex with; how sexuality connects to morality; what relationship there is between pleasurable sex and biological reproduction; who can be paid for sex and who can't; what are the different forms of cash transfer in sex; and what is defined as legal or illegal sex—these are only some of the questions asked by sociologists about sexuality. Sexuality is a chief subject matter for the sociologist because it is socially regulated and because its social regulation is hidden from view—in fact, made invisible. Having sex is a way of performing and reproducing social and cultural structures because sexuality contains responses to such questions as who has power (e.g., a free Greek man would have been viewed as morally inferior if he was penetrated anally by a slave; he had to be the penetrator); what the role of desire is in one's subjectivity (it is given full legitimacy in consumer culture and very little in Christian monastic life); what the proper organizational framework for sexuality is (connubial bedroom, brothel, nightclub, mystery religious cults like those of Bacchus or Dionysus); or what place sexuality has in morality (a mark of depravity in Christian culture or a mark of self-realization in a culture dominated by Freudianism). Sexuality is never just the sheer encounter of two bodies, but also a way of enacting society's social hierarchies and morality (sexual transgressions are no less defined by society, for they make sense only in reference to a norm). That sexuality is always social is true even when, or especially when, it is "free."

Modern sexuality contains quintessential elements of what it means to be a competent and full member of a modern society. First and foremost, sexuality has been one of the central cultural vectors carrying forth the modernist watchword "freedom." Through the influence of Freudian (and post-Freudian) culture, sexuality became crucial for the formation of the self, a site of self-discovery, self-knowledge, and self-realization. It is at once a site to discover and speak about the truth of the self and a site to shape the autonomy of the self. This is the reason why many of the chief dramas of modern selfhood have been scripted as dramas of sexuality—for example, coming of age, coming out of the closet, discovering and being able to achieve multiple orgasms, and, more recently, coming to terms with sexual trauma. Sexuality thus not only is about the autotelic experience of pleasure (for its own sake) with no reference to reproduction; it also stages and mobilizes some key motives of the definition of the good modern self, self-possessed, self-knowing, and hedonist (able to pursue her or his utilities and satisfaction).

The second way in which sexuality is crucial to modern

selfhood lies in the fact that it has been a highly effective tool to socialize individuals into consumer culture, as it demands an unprecedented amount of consumer practices (e.g., "sexiness" demands a perpetual grooming of the body through sport, cosmetics, and fashion; meeting partners demands an ongoing act of consumption in the leisure sphere in bars and restaurants; the sexual act often entails the consumption of sexual aids, toys, and pornography). As a practice in which the body is publicly and privately displayed, modern sexuality represents a crucial site for the formation of the consumer self, defined by its ability to make choices, to pursue one's self-interest, and to undertake pleasurable pursuits.

Sexuality conveys yet a third aspect of modern selfhood. It has become the terrain around which heterosexual and homosexual women and men have redefined the purpose of marriage, love, and reproduction through such notions as equality and consent. Sexuality is thus not only a hedonist project but a political and moral one as well, saturated with the injunction to display ideals of equality and consent.

Sexuality has been the conveyor belt for the cultural "modernization" of men and women, a privileged site for enacting the modernist value of freedom, the ability to exercise consumer choice, and the awareness of rights as equal subjects. In becoming the site for cultural modernity, sexuality also became the site for its characteristic paradoxes and aporias: sexual encounters are regulated by the normative ideals of freedom, autonomy, and an implicitly contractual relationship, in which the freedom of each party is always implicitly kept. In sexuality, two subjectivities must negotiate consent, symmetry, and reciprocity, each retaining his and her right to define or redefine the meaning of the encounter and to leave at any moment. (This is what Anthony Giddens [1991] called the "pure relationship.") But the free and contractual character of modern relations is also what makes them replete with uncertainty: which obligations and commitments, exactly, does sexuality entail? It has become difficult, if not impossible, to say. *Fifty Shades of Grey* articulates the uncertainty that has come to inhere in sexuality. In fact, *Fifty Shades of Grey* encodes the various forms of uncertainty contained in sexuality and resolves them in a relationship of unambiguous romance and love induced by sexuality. Sexuality is not subsequent to love—which made it replete with emotional certainty—but precedes it, and has thus become one more arena of negotiation between two selves. The pleasure of reading this novel—regardless of its poor quality—derives from the fact that it articulates both the set of tensions that plague modern heterosexual relationships and a contemporary utopia of sexual love, resuscitated from the ashes of the conventions of romantic passion and oxymoronically envisioned in a sadomasochistic relationship.

Sexuality: The Great Uncertainty

If a best-seller encodes the social conundrums of its era, what are they in terms of E. L. James's novel? *Fifty Shades of Grey* unfolds as a story line that contains and articulates, in a way that is congruent with the analysis I offered in *Why Love Hurts* (2012), the baffling social experience that structures the romantic and sexual condition. In identifying these conditions, the poor writing of the novel is actually a great help. Its numerous repetitions are precious to the sociologist because they indicate which aspects of the story were intentionally emphasized, and these, in turn, are useful tools in any interpretive strategy attentive to the *intentions* of producers of culture. Following my own interpretive method in *Oprah Winfrey and the Glamour of Misery* (2003), I use intentions as points of entry into a text to identify those meanings that connect a text to a social experience. Novels, like other cultural creations or ordinary speech, make claims, address problems, and attempt to solve them. Repetitions, that is, recurring phrases or insistent meanings, are those that demand that we pay attention to them (this method is opposite to that of deconstruction, which would look for the silences of or absences in a text). My interpretive strategy first identifies the meanings that are explicitly and consciously intended to cater to the readers' expectations, and only then inquires into the conditions to which these meanings unconsciously point.

Serial Sexuality v. Monogamous Love

The first and (to a large extent) second volumes of the *Fifty Shades* trilogy revolve around deciphering the meaning of Christian's voracious sexuality. Such sexuality, however "unconventional," does not elicit in Ana (or in the reader) a clear moral condemnation, only curiosity. This is because Christian's sexuality is set in the background of recreational sexuality: throughout the twentieth century, pleasure was elevated to become the legitimate and self-proclaimed substitute for reproduction as the goal of sexuality, and such sexuality increasingly became an aspect of men's and women's recreational pleasures in general (Laumann et al. [1994] 2000; Rutter and Schwartz 2011). Men's sexuality took an even more decisive turn when it became redefined as a serial sexuality— that is, a sexuality in which sexual experiences are accumulated (synchronically or diachronically). The result has been that sexuality (male in particular) increasingly became distinct from sentiments and love. After sex was separated from matrimony, it moved on toward becoming separated from romantic sentiments.

One illustration of this cultural process was the famous erotic best-seller *Emmanuelle* (Arsan 1971), in which the Italian nobleman Mario initiates the heroine into eroticism's true spirit of freedom by teaching her how to dissociate love from sex. In fact, her entire sexual initiation consists in being able to perform such disconnectedness. Sex for Emmanuelle became an empty and free-floating signifier, detached from its previous signified of love and matrimony. The question that has thus reverberated throughout the mass-mediated literature geared to women for the last few decades is whether sex should be connected back to its "proper" emotional meaning.

Yet the separation of love from sex does not make sexuality into a practice that is free of social determinants. On the contrary, in many ways sexuality continues to be organized under the regime of heteronormativity, defined by Calvin Thomas as "the institution, structures of understanding, and practical orientations that make heterosexuality not only coherent—that is, organised as a sexuality—but also privileged" (2009:21). Sexuality is now detached from its previous institutional referent of matrimony, but it is now organized in and by the consumer market, through which heterosexuality is played out as its dominant model. In this vein, Christian is a prototype of what we may call serial recreational sexuality organized under the aegis of the market. Serial because the text stresses the many partners he has had (his relationship with Ana is always disturbed by his "exes," Elena, Susi, and Leila); he was initiated into sadomasochism at the age of fourteen by an older woman; he has had fifteen "subs" (submissives) and many other sexual partners, dubbed the "club of sub." Recreational because sexuality mimics the consumer leisure market. In fact, here it is developed with the intensity and consumer refinement of an all-consuming hobby, which defines the very identity of the consumer. Christian's practice of BDSM reaches such a level of sophistication and knowledge that it can be said to define his identity in the same way that leisure has become for most the site to express their hidden and true self. In his luxurious apartment, Christian has dedicated an entire room—the Red Room—to sex, and as in the fairy tales, it is kept locked. It contains a vast array of sexual toys, such as shackles, ropes, beads, whips, canes, handcuffs, vibrators, vibrating wands, and butt plugs. Christian is a stylized illustration of the recreational and serial sexuality that came to characterize masculinity throughout the twentieth century. Wealth, social power, sexiness, sexual potency— all these make Christian a man endowed with the attributes of what we may here call hypermasculinity.

Recreational sexuality—precisely because it shifts the social organization of sex from matrimony to the consumer market—has generated cultural anxieties around the question of the male (and increasingly female) capacity to commit— that is, to attach an emotional signified to the signifier of love. These anxieties have been largely encoded in the narrative of *Fifty Shades*, as Ana's inner dialogue (she talks to herself as if she were to herself an outside voice) frequently consists of attempts to decipher Christian's *real* emotions and intentions, that is, his commitment. Their story starts with what must be a typical script for modern serial masculinity: "'I don't do the girlfriend thing,' he says softly." Or again: "'I don't make love. I fuck ... hard ... you don't yet know what you're in for. You could still run for the hills'" (vol. 1). In a conversation with her best friend Kate, Ana declares: "'We don't make love— we fuck—Christian's terminology'" (vol. 1). This can be described as one of the standard beginnings of modern sexual encounters: Ana has undeniable feelings for Christian, anxiously interrogating the nature of Christian's having sex with her; Christian, on the other hand, explicitly declares that sex as such does not engage him or his intentions, emotions, or projects. Christian is, then, quintessentially commitment-phobic (even presumed to be gay because he is never seen in the company of a girlfriend).

The main question that draws the reader into the story is thus the same question that stands squarely at the beginning of many contemporary relationships: Is this "only" sex? Does he want "more" (where feelings are now deemed to be the surplus value of sex)? Is this meaning*ful* or meaning*less*? (Obviously, the gender asking the question can be changed, but women, like Ana, have been the prototypical ones asking it.) Unless sexual encounters are explicitly defined as fleeting and hedonistic, they become fraught with uncertainty, with women often reduced to the (inferior) status of trying to decipher men's intentions and of bringing them to the path of intimacy through sophisticated emotional strategies (learned with the help of guidebooks to relationships, therapy sessions, or advice from women friends). But this will not be an easy task for Ana. Christian is a particularly moody and elusive man: he does only sex; declares himself unfit for love; inflicts pain (lawfully); is sexually aggressive and dominant; and hides a dark secret. The difficulty is increased by Christian's great power: economic (he is fabulously rich), social (his adoptive parents are rich and educated), cultural (he knows how to play classical masterpieces on the piano), and sexual (he is strikingly attractive and exceptionally sexually potent). He is also uncannily aloof and undecipherable. "He's very driven, controlling, arrogant—scary, really, but very charismatic" (as described by Ana in vol. 1). Christian stands for women's modern perception of masculinity: highly ambiguous (difficult to decipher), ambivalent (having mixed feelings), at once caring and menacing, protective and hurtful, vulnerable and powerful. (Men and women could well be equally protective and menacing, but because masculinity holds social power, it is far more threatening than the portrayals of "mad" or "hysterical" women that make up the cultural carnival of threatening women.)

Christian's different psychological facets emerge as the sex between him and Ana morphs into love. In conformity with the genre of romance, Christian relinquishes the secrecy, power, and strength of his masculinity to Ana and turns into an uncommonly devoted lover. As one reader put it: "What I loved [about the second volume] was that it was a great love story" (S. James 2012). The reader's and Ana's anxiety around male commitment is overcome by what turns out to be a display of love far more extravagant and passionate than that of any conventional romantic lover: the threatening and aggressive Christian becomes ceaselessly demonstrative in his declarations of eternal love, his eagerness to marry Ana, to protect her security: to use his helicopter and private jet to accompany her when she leaves town, to hire personnel to protect her physical security, to pay surprise visits to her in remote locations when she travels, and to request that she accompany him on his trips. Christian never tires of her presence, wherever he is and whatever he is doing. For fifteen hundred pages he repeatedly desires her and shows his anxiety about the possibility of losing her or seeing her hurt by others. He slowly morphs from a sadist into a romantic lover, fulfilling a woman's deep fantasy to see the man's formidable power surrender to her love (whether he loves her or stalks her, however, is an open-ended question, left unresolved by the story).

But such "surrender" of male power to the female realm of sentiments entails the risk of weakening his masculinity and sexual potency. Given that a woman is socially defined by her weakness, surrendering to her would mean to display an even greater weakness. This is why in modern societies love poses a complex threat to men's status. Although Christian is drawn into the female sphere of intimacy, he remains endowed with an exceptional sexual drive and power, automatically granted to him by his dominant position in the sexual sadomasochist relationship. Where a Victorian-era man, for example, would have showed his ardor with poetry and chocolates, Christian shows it with vaginal beads, anal sex, and helicopter rides.

What prevents the narrative from collapsing into a monotonous depiction of perfect love and sex is the fact that it switches quickly from symbiosis to separation and to the infliction of mutual pain. "Fiftyness, my husband can be so romantic. I gaze down at the faint marks on my wrist [where he chained her]. Then again, he can be savage sometimes." The expression "Fifty Shades" stands for Christian's moodiness and for the many contrasting ways in which he relates to Ana. "One minute he rebuffs me, the next he sends me fourteen-thousand-dollar books." Or: "His sudden aloofness has left me paralyzed. What happened to the generous, relaxed, smiling man who was making love to me not half-an-hour ago?" Christian's "fiftyness" makes his masculinity both hypermasculine and indeterminate, impossible to fix into a clear set of attributes (or perhaps it is precisely "wild, untamable masculinity" [vol. 3]).

In the same way that Christian is a combination of intense masculine power and feminine longing for emotional symbiosis, Ana takes on attributes of masculine autonomy. Throughout the trilogy, Ana fights tooth and nail for her autonomy, in fact, slowly winning her autonomy through love. As a literary character, Ana has an inner voice that comments on the action, while Christian is perceived through her point of view, indicating that, as a character, she has an autonomy that he does not. Christian never needs "his own space"; Ana does. When they exchange e-mails at work, Ana unfailingly responds: "Please let me concentrate on my work." When a man grabs her on a dance floor, she punches him in the face and preempts Christian's own violent reaction. Ana tells Christian numerous times, "I know how to take care of myself" (vol. 3). This, then, turns out to be a love story in which the man and the woman of the story trade their respective "Mars" and "Venus" qualities: Christian's immense social and sexual power is matched only by his intense and permanent need for symbiosis; Ana's love is tempered by her genuine need for autonomy.

The narrative thus follows a three-pronged movement: it encodes strong gender differences, systematically blurs them in offering us the spectacle of a struggle of two androgynous wills (they constantly fight with each other on the questions of his softness and of her autonomy), and ultimately reconciles these struggles in intense sadomasochistic sex, which reenacts their gender identities and stabilizes their differences, but also makes these differences acceptable because pleasurable (to the characters and to the reader).

Capitalist societies have demanded that men accumulate great economic and social power; sociologically, this has distanced men from the female realm of sentiments and domesticity, made them less likely than their leisurely aristocratic equivalents to be absorbed by poetic and emotional self-expression (Carnes and Griffen 1990). Moreover, because men have embraced cultural models of serial and recreational sexuality to a far greater extent than women, they have become emotionally more detached than women. *Fifty Shades of Grey* encodes such tensions and contradictions between recreational sexuality and love, between men's social power and women's sphere of intimacy and domesticity, and between men's detachment and women's emotional involvement. These tensions are narratively overcome in and by characters who mix gender attributes and are androgynous. It is the play of opposites that takes us properly into the realm of fantasy, defined as a representation that simultaneously encodes reality and denies it.

Desire or Autonomy?

Falling in love entails a loss of sovereignty. In romanticism, it is felt as an exalted and direct experience of passion as a primal and raw force of nature. But in modernity, the loss of sovereignty is a problem, a condition that threatens the integrity of the self because it threatens its autonomy in seeming to surrender to another's will. This is because in modernity autonomy is the master cultural code of selfhood, encoded in the legal and economic spheres and in the realm of psychic well-being. A plethora of psychological discourses aim to provide techniques to learn autonomy by calling on women and men (but mostly women) to approach passion with suspicion and to monitor the mechanism of self-abandonment and self-sacrifice. To that extent, we may say that autonomy and passion have become antithetical. Along this modernist vein, *Fifty Shades of Grey* is a novel about what it means to lose one's sovereignty while pursuing one's autonomy.

In the first volume, Ana and Christian's initial encounter consists in defining very clearly their respective positions ("submissive" and "dominant") and the conditions under which Christian will not lose control. As the contract stipulates: "The Submissive shall serve the Dominant in any way the Dominant sees fit and shall endeavor to please the Dominant at all times to the best of her ability." But Christian wants more than Ana's submission; he wants her to will it: "I want you to willingly surrender yourself to me, in all things," he tells her. Where the "new man" (i.e., the man who has taken heed of feminism) would have said, "I need you" (i.e., an expression of his vulnerability), Christian says instead, "I need you to need me," an expression of a vulnerable *and* imperious masculinity—because for submission to be complete, the dominant must transform the very core of the submissive's desire, making her or him want to subject the self to another's will. As Roger Scruton put it, sadism is "paradoxical" (2006, 13), and this paradox is inherent in desire: we want the object of our desire to also become the object of our will, but we need him to remain a subject, that is, to have an autonomous will and desire, for only a subject can be desired, and only a subject can, in turn, give us the feeling of being truly desired. In that sense, the sadist is in the same paradoxical position as Hegel's Master in his dialectic of the master and the slave: to dominate another means to erase their will; but domination can be truly achieved only if it rules over a free consciousness that recognizes one's lordship. The consciousness that the Master aims to subdue, but that he needs, will eventually become aware of itself, become autonomous, and rebel against the Master.

Indeed, at the end of volume 1 Ana leaves Christian, unwilling to surrender to his "needs" because in the process of negotiating with him about his needs, Ana has become aware of needs of her own, thus affirming her autonomy. This is the explicit reason she invokes for refusing to sign the BDSM contract: "Not sure why this [Clause 2] is solely for MY benefit— i.e., to explore MY sensuality and limits. I'm sure I wouldn't need a ten page contract to do that! Surely this is for YOUR benefit." Autonomy can thus be defined as an awareness of the conditions under which one will not relinquish his or her equality with another. This is the position opposite to that of the masochist, best exemplified by the character of O in Pauline Réage's famous *Story of O* ([1954] 2012), in which the heroine accedes to being whipped, tortured, and defiled for the sake of her love for René. *Story of O* ultimately suggests that the logic of female heterosexual love is masochistic and that such logic leads to the erasure of the self: "She did not wish to die, but if torture was the price she had to pay to keep her lover's love, then she only hoped he was pleased that she had endured it."

Ana, in contrast, leaves Christian despite her love for him, and this act brings the narrative to a Hegelian moment: it compels Christian to "recognize" her, that is, to fall in love with her because of her assertion of autonomy. After one of Christian's "I love you"s, Ana asks, "Despite my disobedience?" Christian replies, "Because of your disobedience" (vol. 2). A relationship that started as Christian's attempt to dominate Ana and turn her into a Sub, a slave, becomes a "struggle for recognition," an endless verbal joust with the Dom progressively submitting to the will of the Sub, resonating with the tales in which the weak (the Sub) turns out to be the truly powerful one (the Dom). (Again, I owe this remark to Dana Kaplan.) Christian relinquishes his will to power and wants instead to be recognized by Ana. "You are one challenging woman, Ana Steele," he says repeatedly and lovingly (vol.1). It is another's autonomy that kindles our own desire and our love—we desire another in his or her autonomy. And our own desire in turn generates another's desire. "One desires the desire of another—even a child knows this" (Brand 2012, 25).

The core of the fantasy of *Fifty Shades of Grey* has to do with the emotional dynamic it depicts: one where the autonomy of Ana and the power of Christian create each other's desire, and one where the submission of the one to the other's will creates further autonomy and desire. As Ana describes: "He clicks something on the bar [where her ankles are attached with cuffs], then pushes, so my legs spread further. Whoa, three feet apart. My mouth drops open, and I take a deep breath. Fuck, this is hot. I'm on fire, restless and needy" (vol. 2).

Ana's desire is here at once submissive and autonomous, further provoking Christian's desire of and his own submission to her: "You never cease to amaze me, Ana. You're so wet," he incessantly repeats.

When he ties her hands after she has a powerful orgasm: "In a daze I do as I'm told. He pulls both my hands backward and cuffs them to the bar, next to my ankles. *Oh ...* My knees are drawn up, my ass in the air, utterly vulnerable, completely his. 'Ana, you look so beautiful.' His voice is full of wonder, and I hear the rip of foil."

These descriptions have the same monotonous structure: her agency is denied, and affirmed in the very movement of being denied, because her autonomy creates his desire, which makes her vulnerable, which in turn generates his vulnerability; through the exertion of his power, he subjects her to him but becomes in that movement subjugated by and to her, furthering her own autonomy.

As philosopher Roy Brand notices, "the stability of this system [of desire] is always at risk, for I cannot possess the desire of another. The offering of desire must be mutual, circular, and self-supporting: I desire your desire desiring my desire and so on" (2012, 74). This dynamic is not only circular but highly fragile. Desire, autonomy, negotiation, reciprocity, and equality are forces that push and pull relationships in directions that are very difficult to predict. This is why romantic relationships have become unpredictable, or "chaotic," in Ulrich Beck and Elisabeth Beck-Gernsheim's (2002) felicitous formulation. But in *Fifty Shades*, Christian's power and Ana's autonomy do not create chaos, that is, a dynamic process in which each moves away from the other; instead, it generates their own and the other's perpetual desire.

> And suddenly the nature of his kiss alters, no longer sweet, reverential, and admiring, but carnal, deep, and devouring— his tongue invading my mouth, taking not giving, his kiss possessing a desperate, needy edge. As desire courses through my blood, awakening every muscle and sinew in its wake, I feel a frisson of alarm. *Oh Fifty, what's wrong?* He inhales sharply and groans. "Oh, what you do to me," he murmurs, lost and raw. He moves suddenly, lying down on top of me, pressing me into the mattress–one hand cupping my chin, the other skimming over my body, my breast, my waist, my hip, and around my behind. He kisses me again, pushing his leg between mine, raising my knee, and grinding against me, his erection straining against our clothes and my sex. (vol. 3)

The novel fulfills a modern type of fantasy, which is *not* that of eternal or perfect love; on the contrary, Ana and Christian's love seems constantly fraught with struggles and negotiations. The powerful fantasy they enact is one in which the struggle over autonomy and power does not conflict with desire but generates it. In that sense, the novel manages to resolve the fundamental tension of desire in modernity by making the normally opposed logic of desire and autonomy closely interlocked. As Ana herself says: "It's very confusing being with you. You don't want me to defy you, but then you like my 'smart mouth.' You want obedience, except when you don't, so you can punish me. I just don't know which is up when I'm with you'" (vol. 1). While the imperative of autonomy in the real world of real relationships is an obstacle to relationships because it creates distance in the autono-

mous person and uncertainty in the desiring person, this conundrum has been here resolved: "I like defying you," Ana
says, to which Christian responds: "'I know. And it's made me
so . . . happy.' He smiles down at me through his bemusement"
(vol. 3). While the dynamic of desire is normally opposed to
autonomy (desire makes the subject vulnerable and depen-
dant), desire here only feeds the project of autonomy in a tele-
ological movement that comes to reinforce the very meaning
of heteronormativity. Indeed, as some scholars have argued,
heteronormative sex is sex with a purpose, with a story, with
a goal (marriage, love, shared life, a child). It is, in short, sex
with an identity, as opposed precisely to the kind of sex of
demonstrated by O, which is ultimately to dissolve the self.

Winning the Struggle for Recognition

Modern societies produce a chronic deficit in recognition, or
the capacity to be backed up by others in our sense of value
and self-worth (Fraser and Honneth 2003). Indeed, as I argued in *Why Love Hurts*, recognition has become one of the
central problems of modern romantic relationships, and this
new sociological characteristic is explicitly encoded in *Fifty
Shades*. Ana's inner voice is replete with self-doubts with regard to her worth. "Romantically, though, I've never put myself out there, ever. A lifetime of insecurity—I'm too pale, too
skinny, too scruffy, uncoordinated, my long list of faults goes
on," she tells herself in volume 1. Well into volume 3 of the trilogy, she is incessantly surprised to be loved by Christian and
to have been chosen by the most eligible bachelor in Seattle.
"I just don't get why he likes me," she says in volume 2. "I have
never understood why he likes me."

As Ana illustrates, insecurity has become intrinsic to the romantic condition because sexual encounters are now socially

organized in the form of a market in which men and women compete with other members of the same group along various dimensions of status, wealth, education as well as beauty and attractiveness. This marketlike situation of competition (made even more obvious in the Internet medium, in which competitors are actually seen and arrayed as if on a buffet table) has become especially acute in the sexual realm and thus creates chronic insecurity and the need for recognition in this realm. While we know little about Ana's "objective" beauty, we do know that her roommate, Kate, is very beautiful, smart, poised, well dressed, and from a very good family background. Ana is the quintessential Miss Everybody. She does not know how to dress, comes from an ordinary family, is poorly coordinated and clumsy, does not have Kate's savvy and wealth. Her ordinariness strengthens the fantasy power of the narrative, because it makes her similar to all women who secretly dread not being unique or outstanding enough. Yet it is Ana—the ordinary and the clumsy—who is chosen by Christian, thus turning her into a feminine Horatio Alger; this becomes a story of romantic self-made success through spirit and character. This novel, which contains so much about sexuality and sex, is in fact about the victory of old-fashioned "character" over beauty and sexiness.

Similarly, we progressively discover that Christian's childhood trauma has filled him with self-loathing and an incapacity to feel loved. In a telling dialogue in volume 2, Ana says to him: "You're very easy to love. Don't you see that?"

Christian replies: "No, baby, I don't."

Ana: "You are. And I do and so does your family. . . . you are worthy."

His answer is "I can't hear this. I'm nothing, Anastasia. I'm a husk of a man. I don't have a heart."

Elsewhere Ana tells herself: "My heart clenches because I

know; it's because he's so doubting, so full of self-loathing"
(vol. 2).

In other words, both characters are crippled with a sense
that they lack self-worth.

Implausibly, talking to Dr. Flynn, Christian's psychoana-
lyst, Ana tells him: "Part of me thinks that if he [Christian]
wasn't this broken he wouldn't ... want me."

Dr. Flynn's eyebrows shoot up in surprise: "That's a very
negative thing to say about yourself, Ana. And frankly it says
more about you than it does about Christian. It's not quite up
there with his self-loathing, but I'm surprised by it."

As one of Christian's ex-lovers—Elena—repeats, the powerful Christian is full of self-loathing and fear that Ana will
leave him as soon as she learns of his dark past and true origins. The motif of "the madwoman in the attic" (Gilbert and
Gubar [1979] 2000), which characterized the gothic novel
(e.g., *Jane Eyre*), has been replaced by a narrative of trauma in
which the self and its sense of worth are what is actually hidden. The attic has moved to the interiority of the characters in
the form of a trauma narrative. Christian's trauma makes him
at once aloof (Ana is not allowed to touch his chest, for reasons Ana and the reader do not understand) and vulnerable.
The narrative thus deliberately encodes what has become a
crucial dimension of romantic relationships, namely the fact
that men and women play out dramas of self-worth in them
and through them.

In the same movement, however, the novel offers a stag-
gering number of examples of ways in which each cures the
other's insecurity and lack of self-worth. "He stares at me with
adoring wonder, and I am sure I mirror his expression as I
reach up to caress his beautiful face" (vol. 2). No superlative
is spared. "In all things, Anastasia. You are a siren, a goddess"
(vol. 2). The end of the process is nothing less than a complete

cure from the dark past that has tormented Christian. While symbolic and physical violence often leave indelible traces—bodily or psychic—here love manages to undo the inscription of symbolic violence in the body and self and to provide what philosopher Simon May (2011) calls "ontological groundedness," a sense of being at home in the world.

One of the fantasies performed in the novel is that our ordinariness can become our uniqueness when our inner worth is affirmed through love. Love allows us to win, so to speak, over the competition with others, to become unique, differentiated, distinct. At the end of this process, Christian has found nothing less than a complete psychological overhaul. In volume 2 he says: "My whole attitude has changed as a result. My whole outlook on life has radically shifted." The ultimate fantasy of recognition is to be selected by one person and in that process to be transformed, healed from what Pierre Bourdieu (1991) calls the symbolic violence of the social order. It is doubtful whether love can ever fully substitute for such social recognition, but it does offer a powerful hope that it can.

The Problem with Equality, or "Just Fucking Fuck Me, Already"

Feminism is no longer only a political movement but has also become a cultural code, used in advertising, TV series, movies, and romance novels (Cantor 1988; Freeman 2001). Affirming this cultural code often involves nothing more than paying lip service to the moral force and political demands of feminism and has even made feminism lose its political edge, becoming an empty gesture (McRobbie 1991).

This cultural code of feminism has transformed the ways in which gender, sexuality, and the family are portrayed in mass media. My point is *not* that *Fifty Shades* is a feminist book (it obviously isn't, because it does not offer an alternative to traditional heteronormativity), but rather that its narrative structure and characters have self-consciously incorporated the feminist cultural code, much like many other areas of popular culture. The critiques of the book as being antifeminist have entirely missed the point, but readers have not failed to noticed the presence of the feminist code: "The book actually keeps its female protagonist in charge of everything that happens in the bedroom. She has the power. The couple in *50 Shades* only pretends to be slave and master. Anastasia is actually the one setting the rules (she renegotiates the sex contract on just about every page) and Christian accedes to all her wishes" (Liner 2012).

Anastasia Steele is an almost parodic model of assertiveness: she always knows quickly and clearly what her emotional needs are (emotional needs are by definition elusive); she coolly and competently rebuffs the psychological and physical aggression of Christian's ex-lovers; she threatens to fire a woman who looks at her attractive husband too insistently. She refuses to change her name when they get married; she punches a man who grabs her in a discotheque; she refuses to benefit from any advantage that Christian's position as owner of the publishing company in which she works would give her. She insists on treating him when they go out, despite his extravagant wealth; she insists on going out to meet her friends, despite the danger to her physical security; she shoots guns. And far from least, she proves herself to be a highly competent and liberated sexual partner. In short, Ana is the model of assertiveness envisioned by feminism, and it is as such that she has been self-consciously encoded in the narrative.

Feminism is a radical movement in the etymological sense

of that word: it went to the very root of women's social being and tried to transform the very nature of their own (and
men's) desire. While feminism's claim to economic equality (same pay for same work) does not meet with significant
moral objections any longer, the attempt to reform the structure of heterosexual desire has met with opposition even from
women who otherwise espouse the call to economic equality. While feminism has made progress in the workplace (de-
manding equal pay and representation in positions of lead-
ership), women have become ever more sexualized in the
consumer and media spheres, further deepening the grip of
men's control and women's own resistance to feminism. The
sexualization of women's identity has been incessantly pro-
moted through the images of the sexed, sexualized, and sexy
body, which has successfully performed its sexualized femininity through sex with men and through the intensive use
of consumer culture (for an illustration of this, see *Sex and
the City*). It is through sex and sexuality that women are made
to perform a simulacrum of their emancipation. Why then,
have sexuality and desire proved to be such reluctant arenas
for women's equality?

In a much-discussed article about *Fifty Shades of Grey*, Katie Roiphe makes a further claim: " To a certain, I guess, rather
large, population, it [*Fifty Shades of Grey*] has a semiporno-
graphic glamour, a dangerous frisson of boundary crossing, but
at the same time is delivering reassuringly safe, old-fashioned
romantic roles" (2012). Roiphe continues: "In the realm of
private fantasy, the allure of sexual submission, even in its ex-
tremes, is remarkably widespread. An analysis of 20 studies
published in *Psychology Today* estimates that between 31 percent and 57 percent of women entertain fantasies where they
are forced to have sex." Quoting Daphne Merkin from the
New Yorker (February 1996), Roiphe further muses: "Equal-

ity between men and women, or even the pretext of it, takes a lot of work and may not in any case be the surest route to sexual excitement." Roiphe here echoes an increasingly loud litany lamenting the fact that equality has brought the demise of sexual desire (forcefully exposed, for example, in Cristina Nehring's successful *A Vindication of Love*). Equality, critics claim, is not very sexy because it demands consent, negotiation, which is another way to say that it demands procedures. Men who have learned the lessons of feminism lack sexual directness and vigor; women long for a form of masculinity that is more stylized, sure of itself, and playful. But this only pushes further the question, why is traditional masculinity pleasurable in fantasy? In other words, why are some of women's fantasies still caught in patriarchy?

The premodern bonds between men and women were based on what we may call metaphorically a feudal social system: men dominated women; that is, men received women's sexual and domestic services in exchange for which men granted women their (presumed) protection. The traditional men provided economically for his dependents (women and children) and defended them with his body. This unequal social system was based on a bond of reciprocal dependence. Inequality— translated into protectiveness—thus contained undeniable forms of pleasure, an important one being the *clarity* of the gender roles it implied. In contrast, equality is intrinsically more muddled because it cannot fix roles or values to roles. In that sense, equality is less pleasurable because it generates uncertainty and ambivalence.

The second pleasure found in inequality is that in translating power into protectiveness, it creates a "natural" mutual dependency and thick emotional glue. Equality, on the contrary, does not create a sense of obligation but rather an awareness of each one's own needs and rights, which can potentially conflict with the rights and needs of the other. The moral claims made by equality are thus by definition less emotionally binding to another.

The third pleasure found in inequality resides in the fact that when they are not negotiated, roles generate emotions that are more spontaneous and immediate, because well-scripted social roles do not require negotiation or even reflexiveness, a capacity to reflect on the relation itself while it is unfolding. Egalitarian norms unscript roles and identities and turn relationships into entities that must be negotiated through "communication." As a blog writer put it: "It's become generally accepted that communication is the key to good sex—communication tips have become a cornerstone of sex guides for everyone from *Christian couples* to *sex slaves*. But talking can be difficult, and maybe the popularity of *50 Shades* is in part a backlash against the admonishment to talk, a sign that sometimes people yearn for someone who just *knows*" (North 2012). A Seattle woman expressed this sentiment in a Craigslist (2008) ad that went viral, under the heading "Just fucking fuck me, already." And so did Jessa, of *Girls*: when a man she picked up in a bar asked if it was okay to put his hand in her pants, she responded, "Never ask me that again in my whole life." "Maybe *50 Shades of Grey* speaks to *women's desire not to have to speak*" (North). What this reader refers to as "not to have to speak" is another way of saying "not to have to negotiate," where negotiation results from the fact that women are responsible for preserving a state of pragmatic and emotional equality with their partners.

I would argue, then, that the backlash against feminism is a longing for patriarchy, not because women long for domination per se but because they long for the emotional bonds and glue that accompanied, hid, justified, and made domination invisible, as if one could separate male protectiveness from the feudal system of domination in which men granted such protectiveness. In other words, modern femininity has to face the still widely prevalent power of males, minus the feudal code of protectiveness that regulated the inferior status of women. This is why the narrative of *Fifty Shades* articulates an archetypal masculinity: it is in fact a protective masculinity, reminiscent of what I have just called feudal masculinity.

Examples abound: "They want what is mine," Christian says about Ana's potential suitors. "'Mine' he repeats, his eyes glowing possessively" (vol. 2). Or on the day of their wedding: "With infinite slowness, he unfastens each button, all the way down my back. 'I love you so much.' Trailing kisses from the nape of my neck to the edge of my shoulder. Between each kiss he murmurs, 'I.Want.You.So.Much.I.Want.To.Be. Inside. You. You. Are. Mine'" (vol. 3). Or when they decide to get married, on the day of the ceremony, Ray—Ana's stepfather—tells Christian: "Look after my girl, Christian," Christian replies, "I fully intend to, Ray." In a typical male *rite de passage*, Ana enters matrimony with one protective man passing her to another protective man. And thus, despite his immense wealth, Christian refuses to have Ana sign a pre-nup—a testimony to his capacity to subscribe to a nonmodern, that is, a noncontractual, marriage.

The male gesture that is fantasized about here and that is performed by Christian throughout the three novels is noncontractual protectiveness accompanied by moral equality. Such acts of protection and possessiveness are too frequent not to mean something important. They reflect the ambivalence of many women vis-à-vis the ways in which feminism has transformed traditional masculinity and femininity and the relation of the sexes into a contractual bond. I would argue that such ambivalence is not due to the fact that feminism has stripped away love from its mystique (this is the claim made by detractors of feminism) but rather from the fact that the feminist revolution has remained selective (affecting more women than men) and unfinished (the economic sphere and the family are still largely patriarchal). It is the selectiveness and the unfinished character of the feminist revolution that have made intimate and sexual relations so fraught with difficulties. The longing for the sexual domination of men is not a longing for their social domination as such. Rather, it is a longing for a mode of sociality in which love and sexuality did not produce anxiety, negotiation, and uncertainty.

So insistent is Christian's protectiveness that it becomes a feminist question self-consciously raised in the story itself: is his protectiveness a form of control and even stalking? Ana refuses to be controlled but slowly discovers through her sexuality that yielding to the domination of another is pleasurable. The apprenticeship works if her autonomy is accompanied by the apprenticeship of her submissiveness. The narrative of *Fifty Shades* is thus able to encode in the character of Ana simultaneously her hyperassertiveness, her self-emancipation through sexuality, and her sexual submissiveness to a male's power and protectiveness.

Christian harbors a form of hyperprotectiveness that is both the sign of traditional masculinity and its justification. His protectiveness is here disconnected from the legal, moral, and cultural order that disenfranchised women. This protectiveness is symbolically pleasurable because it is connected to the modern categorical imperative to experience daily multiple orgasms. Christian Grey combines the ultracommitted traditional patriarch with the sexual athlete who knows and cultivates all the nooks and crannies of women's bodies and female sexuality. In that sense, the fantasy that is at the core of the story is a prime example of "false consciousness": it mixes the emotional power of the traditional patriarch—economically powerful and sexually dominant—with the playful, multi-orgasmic, intensely pleasurable, and autotelic sexuality that is the hallmark of feminist sexual politics.

EPILOGUE / Sadomasochism as a Romantic Utopia

A novel not only organizes into a story social positions and tensions but implicitly articulates a political point of view, which either justifies or questions these positions and tensions. Romance or murder mystery novels address, even if obliquely, social arrangements, hierarchies, and thus provide a way to make sense of the experiences they produce. In this respect, we may ask, what are the normative and political implications of *Fifty Shades of Grey*? Does its focus on BDSM foster a debased view of morality, sexuality, and women?

Before I address this question, a preliminary observation is in order: the "politics" or morality of popular culture is scrutinized more often than that of "high" culture, especially when it concerns sexuality, which is probably the most patrolled topic of Western civilization. This is because sexuality is a chief arena through which government and class domination is exercised, by both conservative and liberal elites (Snitow, Stansell, and Thompson 1983). Conservatives typically want to exercise control through a scrutiny of the birth rate of lower or immigrant populations, through regulation of teenage pregnancy and gay marriage, and through stricter obscenity laws. They thus want to control whatever threatens the integrity of the heterosexual family as a pillar for the transmission of tradition, social reproduction, and education. Liberal, feminist, and neo-Marxists critics, on the other hand, worry about the cultural structures that may reproduce and legitimize (male, heteronormative) domination, the male gaze and point of view, and the commodification of sexuality for the profit of corporations. The question these remarks raise, then, is, how should we differentiate between preoccupation with the politics of a text and the many ways in which sexuality is variously controlled by conservative or liberal elites?

This brings us to the need to make another distinction. The question about the politics of a text needs to be differentiated from the need to order, hierarchize, and allocate a moral valence to cultural behavior. While this moral impulse is an important one, sociologists and cultural analysts should resist it. The prime task of the scholar is to draw the terms of a debate, to think imaginatively about the categories that inhere in a problem; such a task is far from being neutral, but it is different from an evaluation of a cultural object according to its moral or political valence. It is the task of citizens to recode in clear moral and political terms such analysis. In the following, my intent is to clarify the terms of the debate about *Fifty Shades* and about BDSM sexuality, with the hope that it helps us narrow these terms in discussions about the politics of the text, rather than simply repeating various forms of moral controls of sexuality, whether from the right or from the left.

BDSM, or The New Romantic Order

Interest in SM started with sexologists and psychoanalysts who viewed it as a pathology (Weinberg 2006, 18). Freud viewed it as a perversion; some even viewed it as close to cannibalism, necrophilia, or vampirism. But even if we do not pathologize SM, masochism remains a sociological and psychological puzzle. As an Internet psychologist aptly put it: "The self is developed to avoid pain, but masochists seek pain. The self strives for control, but masochists seek to relinquish control. The self aims to maximize its esteem, but masochists deliberately seek out humiliation" (Hayden 2012). Masochism is indeed a voluntary submission and acceptance of pain that radically conflicts with the definition of modern selfhood as self-possessed, autonomous, and hedonist. Why then do women enjoy reading a fiction that stages the voluntary infliction and acceptance of pain?

In a way, the very notion of masochism contains an answer to this question, the masochist being defined by his/her irrational desire for his or her own suffering, and precisely by his or her capacity to convert it into pleasure. Scholars contend that some forms of gothic fiction (*Story of O*, for example, and *Rebecca*) are an aestheticized form of masochism through which women internalize and accept the victim position. For Michelle Massé (1992), through gothic fiction women rehearse the suffering they experience in their sexual and emotional relationships with men. Fiction then teaches and helps anticipate a social position and a social role, by making the painful aspects of relationships between women and men into a pleasurable element of the narrative. Masochism here is not a lifestyle choice or a sexual perversion but rather a socially constructed position that women learn to desire by masking the pain of loving elusive or unavailable men.

If there is an originality and appeal to *Fifty Shades*, it lies in its making entirely explicit the masochism that was left implicit in the gothic formula. In *Fifty Shades*, masochism becomes a stake in the relationship of the two protagonists, an explicit political/moral question, and a source of erotic pleasure for the protagonists and reader. Following Fredric James-on's (1975) famous claim that a narrative genre contains imag-inary resolutions to real social contradictions and conflicts, I suggest that the BDSM relationship between Ana and Chris-tian functions narratively as a resolution of the tensions in-herent in modern heterosexuality, which—as argued above—have been largely encoded in the story. A narrative formula gives shape to socially determined contradictions (e.g., "mar-riage of love v. marriage of interest," or "sexual freedom" and "emotional stability"), because most narratives must bring to a resolution the tensions they contain and articulate imagi-nary ways of transcending and negating these contradictions.

To get a sense of the meaning of the SM sex in the narra-tive of *Fifty Shades of Grey*, we can briefly compare the novel to the famous 1954 *Story of O*, written by Pauline Réage. Like *Fifty Shades*, *Story of O* was written by a heterosexual woman (Reage seems to have written the novel to please her lover Jean Paulhan). O is taken to a chateau by her lover, René, where masked men whip her and abuse her sexually (with O's and her lover's consent). O is elaborately trained to be a sexual slave (e.g., she is made to carry a large piece of wood in her va-gina because she is "too narrow"); her body is made available to men whom she does not know or see. Later in the narrative, René wants her to be always available to him and to receive his sexual assaults, and as an ultimate proof of his domination, he wants her to serve sexually a man she does not love. She finds this man in the person of Stephen, who further advances her training as a sex slave by teaching her not to feel love. O's masochism takes its initial source in her love for René, but she discovers that anonymous sex with other men provides her a greater source of pleasure and desire: "She had moaned be-neath the lips of the stranger as never her lover had made her moan, cried out under the impact of a stranger's member as never her lover had made her cry out. She felt debased and guilty. She could not blame him if he were to leave her." This discovery progressively empties O of her volition: "Beneath the gazes, beneath the hands, beneath the sexes that defiled her, the whips that rent her, she lost herself in a delirious absence from herself which restored her to love and, perhaps, brought her to the edge of death. She was anyone, anyone at all, any one of the other girls, opened and forced like her, girls whom she saw being opened and forced, for she did see it, even when she was not obliged to have a hand in it." *Story of O* stages an affinity that fascinated French intellectuals after World War II, that between eroticism and death, which Georges Bataille (1986) characterized as the desire to become one with humanity, to cease to be an individual clearly individuated and separate from others. Susan Sontag (quoted by Roiphe) drives the point home: for her, O is about "the voluptuous yearning toward the extinction of one's consciousness."

But a simpler and more feminist interpretation of *Story of O* is that women can experience undiluted sexual pleasure and desire, detached from love, only in a state of abjection. In bringing masochism to its logical end—the death of O—the novel unwillingly reveals that at the heart of heterosexual love is the annihilation of women as desiring subjects. In a way, then, *Story of O* shows that in the extinction of one's consciousness, masochism and love form a single continuous chain.

Nothing could be further from the affirmation of subjectivity contained in the struggle to recognize each other as equal partners in the relationship Ana and Christian have in *Fifty Shades*. Theirs is a sexuality that incessantly affirms rather than denies Ana's needs, volition, and subjectivity in the form of a narrative of self-discovery and romantic intimacy. More generally, from a cultural and sociological perspective, an intensification of norms of autonomy, equality, and freedom have gone hand in hand with the increasing normalization and spread of SM practices, with as much as 10 percent of the US population engaging in it by 1990, more still by 1994.[1] That is, viewed as a cultural practice, for the last three or four decades SM has not been opposed to increasing norms of autonomy and self-possession. BDSM has accompanied the development of feminism and greater, rather than lesser, gender equality, thus suggesting that BDSM reflects the shift of sexuality to the realm of identity politics based on a vision of human rights and values that pertain to self-realization. Mirroring these sociological facts, in the novel BDSM accompanies the incessant struggle of Ana and Christian to achieve an egalitarian relationship, with the increasing assertiveness of Ana. The BDSM relationship unfolds along with Ana's subjectivity as an equal desiring subject. In that sense, *Fifty Shades* is part and parcel of that feminine culture so aptly described by Lauren Berlant as a culture in which "true feeling ... sanctifies suffering as a relay to universality" (2008, 12).

BDSM, then, offers a number of symbolic strategies to overcome the dilemmas of the heterosexual struggle that characterizes Ana and Christian's relationship. Here are three such strategies.

1. A National Coalition for Sexual Freedom article quotes the 1990 *Kinsey Institute New Report on Sex*: "Researchers estimate that 5–10 percent of the U.S. population engages in sadomasochism for sexual pleasure on at least an occasional basis, with most incidents being either mild or staged activities involving no real pain or violence" (Reinisch and Beasley 1990, 162–63). Barker, Iantaffi, and Gupta write that "Janus and Janus (1994) report that up to 14% of American men and 11% of American women have engaged in some form of BDSM sexual behavior and estimates of the extent of BDSM fantasy are much higher" (2008, 108).

From Role Confusion to Clarity

Current heterosexuality is pushed and pulled between still powerful norms of heteronormativity and an assault on gender roles and identities. Modern societies demand that men and women trade their identities in the realms of both work and domesticity, to become androgynous, and to break the core of each solid gender identity. Christian and Ana, for example, progressively trade many of their respective gender attributes. In BDSM, on the other hand, roles are reestablished, but in a way that does not necessarily overlap with gender. Indeed, according to some studies powerful men are often those likely to take the masochist's position in a BDSM relationship (Baumeister 1989; Kate 2011; Masters, Johnson, and Kolodny 1995). Thus BDSM avoids the confusion and ambivalence inherent in gender equality and reaffirms sharply defined and stylized sexual roles, yet without predicating them on "hard" gender identities. In fixing clear roles detached from identities, BDSM provides the certainty that comes with scripted roles without returning to traditional gender inequality. This is because whatever inequality is enacted in BDSM is playful rather than inscribed in a social ontology of the sexes. What is played out in BDSM is precisely the radical capacity of subjects to detach a role or position from a sexual ontology. This in turn enables women to imagine Ana's pain through fantasy without the humiliation that usually accompanies the infliction of pain.

Transforming Psychic Suffering into Physical Pain

As I have argued elsewhere,[2] a diffuse form of psychic suffering permeates modern romantic relations through anxiety,

2. See Illouz 2012.

uncertainty, ambivalence, boredom, and the difficulty of reconciling the conflicting imperatives of autonomy and attachment. The struggle for recognition between the sexes often remains inconclusive—that is, it has no victorious denouement. BDSM brings an interesting twist to that struggle: it translates psychic suffering into the certainty of physical pain, but it transmutes it, so to speak, into sexual play, desire, and pleasure, thus giving suffering and pain clear and distinct physical and psychic statuses and boundaries. BDSM puts pain into form, that is, aestheticizes it, thus enabling a distancing from and a control over the experience. Indeed, in BDSM pain follows a protocol: it uses ritualized gestures and familiar devices, follows a scripted gradation, and, most crucially, can be stopped or exited at will (with a code or safe word).

Thus what the act of SM may paradoxically stage is not suffering so much as suffering's capacity to transmute into pleasure, more clear than diffuse and, perhaps mostly, more controlled by the subject, to be stopped on demand. The sadist and the masochist have in common their control of pain—both inflicted and felt—and that control might be what the sufferer secretly desires. That is, what the masochist is actually rehearsing is the *cessation* of pain, which signals in turn the love and care of, or contractual relation with, the sadist. Havelock Ellis, studying masochism, suggested a distinction between masochism as "pain only" and masochism as inflicted by the masochist's desire "to experience pain, but he generally desires that it should be inflicted in love" ([1903] 1926, 160). Sexual sadism and masochism based upon mutual pleasure experienced through receiving/giving pain from/to a loved one became the civilizing principle of sadism and masochism, and remains the framework upon which any "harm" caused through consensual BDSM is "permitted, justified and de-pathologised" (Dymock 2012, 57).

Overcoming the Aporia of Desire

Modern relationships are pure relationships based on consent. But this consent is twice aporetic. For one, as Roger Scruton suggests, desire is divided between "the desire to compel the other to give what is required" and "the compulsion towards agreement, towards the mutual recognition that only what is given can be genuinely received" (2006, 301). Consent cannot by definition address the question of the desire that must be "freely given," thus leaving consensual relationships unable to cope with that aspect of desire that precisely cannot be agreed upon. No matter how much we agree on the conduct of daily life, on what you should give me, I can never secure your desire. This aporetic question is central to women's culture, in which "questions about what counts as emotional reciprocity matter tremendously" (Berlant 2008, 16). How does one create freely given desire in an otherwise perfectly consensual relationship? This question can never be addressed by consensuality itself and, in fact, plagues sexual and romantic relationships. BDSM, on the other hand, while based on consent, does not demand "freely given" desire, because desire becomes subsumed under its theatrical mise-en-scène. The question of how much one desires the other becomes irrelevant. In contrast to the anxiety of normative sexual relationships (e.g., "The 10 Secrets Women Must Know about Men's Sexuality" or "How to Make Her Beg for More"), BDSM formalization is anxiety-free.

Moreover, consent is always partial, because when entering a sexual or romantic relationship, one never knows the full range of behaviors and sentiments one has consented to. In that sense, the consent that is at the heart of heterosexual relationships is illusory. It is a consent to something we never fully know in advance and agree to: did I really consent to the full implications of your careless and withdrawn character? What partners do agree about has become precisely an object of contention. BDSM—and the elaborate contract Christian wants Ana to sign—takes consent far more seriously, for it defines and stages carefully the parameters of the experience one will engage in. In that sense, BDSM is a pure form of consent, without all that was left unagreed and unscripted in "pure relationships," based on the unending negotiations of daily life.

Let me summarize this: one way to characterize our romantic condition is to say that the autonomization of sexuality has made the realm of emotional interactions uncertain, replete with ambivalence about the rules to negotiate commitment, love, and desire. In the language of sociologists, it has become indeterminate. *Fifty Shades of Grey* has encoded this indeterminacy; more exactly, its narrative oscillates "between indeterminacy and determinacy" (Müller and von Groddeck n.d.): the indeterminacy of current romantic relationships and the determinacy of the roles and positions of SM sex.

Self-Help Eroticism

I will go one step further than Jameson—who did not examine women's literature—and claim that some narratives are not only symbolic rehearsals of social dilemmas and of the solution to these dilemmas: they are also performative structures offering ways of acting and doing. The power of *Fifty Shades*—like that of a great deal of women's literature—is not only to encode the conundrums of heterosexuality but also to provide tools to actually make it better. As Linda Williams puts it, pornographic movies are "the solution to the problem of sex through the performance of sex" (1989, 147). We may similarly say that the BDSM of *Fifty Shades* is the solution to the problem of heterosexual relations through a narrative formula that is efferent, with something to carry over into daily life. In that sense, the novel is less pornographic than it is a self-help book.

A pornographic book is defined by the fact that its explicit intent is to make the reader engage in masturbatory practices. Pornographic texts are intended explicitly to arouse sexually, usually, a male and solitary viewer (Garlick 2011, 306–20). They expose genitalia and use words, postures, and narrative devices whose entire purpose is to create sexual desire in the absence of a real partner. (The partner[s] may, of course, be present, but the pornographic narrative is written *as if* the partner[s] were absent.) *Fifty Shades*, on the other hand, is written assuming the presence of a partner. The sexual scenes are not written to arouse the eye but meant to instruct men and women on inventive and efficient ways to improve their sexual pleasure. The following is but one example among many.

"What's with the no going to the bathroom thing?" Ana asks Christian before they start engaging in sex.

> "You really want to know?" He half smiles, his eyes alight with a salacious gleam.
> "Do I?" I gaze at him through my lashes as I take a sip of my wine.
> "The fuller your bladder, the more intense your orgasm, Ana." (vol. 3)

This rather unarousing explanation suggests that what distinguishes this book from conventional erotic novels is that its purpose is not to arouse the solitary reader; rather, it is to invite women to "carry away something" (Rosenblatt's term), and this "something" is a greater fluency in the art of making love, resonating with much sex advice to be found in women's magazines. This fluency is both in the gestures one should use to increase orgasm and in the use of erotic toys. An example:

> "We're going to have some fun with this" he whispers.
> *Fuck!*
> His finger continues down over my perineum and slowly slides into me.... I groan and he eases his finger in and out of me, over and over. I push back on his hand, relishing the intrusion.... "I think you love being here, like this. Mine."
> *I do—oh, I do.* He withdraws his finger and smacks me hard once more. "Tell me," he whispers, his voice hoarse and urgent.
> "Yes, I do," I whimper. (vol. 3)

The other aspect of "self-help eroticism" is to be found in the novel's abundant references to sex toys and to the great care with which these toys are mentioned, with attention paid to their actual use. This hypothesis is largely confirmed by the spectacular increase of sales of sex toys in the United States after the publication of the first *Fifty Shades* volume. Sex toys are a far more significant aspect of feminine sexuality and are viewed as "aids" to sexuality rather than as direct objects of erotic desire. The abundant references to sex toys in the book, then, seems to suggest that the book's portrayal of sexuality is essentially what I would characterize as a "do-it-yourself eroticism."

Claire Cavanah, cofounder of the Manhattan sex shop Babeland, said after the final book in the trilogy was released in the United States in January 2012 that customers "were asking for specific toys that they had read about," but when the trilogy was rereleased in April, "the product sales started to really spike." Since then, Cavanah has noticed a sevenfold increase in demand for a particular sex toy featured in a scene between

Christian and Ana. The store also sells special *Fifty Shades* kits and hosts *Fifty Shades*–themed workshops that teach (mostly female) attendees how to use the toys, but Cavanah said that that was not the only curiosity: "They also just want to get together and see each other."

Fans have also been offered *Fifty Shades*–themed fashions and accommodations, and more recently, an official music album, *Fifty Shades of Grey: The Classical Album*, featuring Bach and Chopin, is the only spinoff item James has so far endorsed (Burzynski 2012). (One has to wonder, though, why the author seems to endorse so wholeheartedly a model of the high culture that her book so patently flouts.)

If the industry has responded so swiftly to the readers and to their interpretation of the *Fifty Shades* narrative, it is because it is written as a self-help narrative, an invitation to change and improve one's sexual life by mimicking the toys-induced orgasms of Ana. This finding is entirely congruent with Janice Radway's analysis of "middle-brow" literature (Radway 1997, 6), which is characterized by an orientation to self-help, and I would suggest that this is because these narratives closely mimic biographical narratives of the quest of self, identity, and self-help staged and encoded by modern culture. Women read books "in highly concrete, deeply resonant ways as persons moving through life in embodied form" (ibid., 14). Such a use of novels stands at the opposite end of the "ideology of the solitary reader" (Long 1992, 104–30), an ideology that stipulates that the activity of reading is detached from the rest of society and consists in the meeting of an author's unique mind with the self-enclosed mind of the reader. It also differs from male eroticism, which is more oriented toward solitary masturbatory practices. Women's reading is often an essentially social activity, both in the sense that books are read with others and in the sense that such reading makes people reflect about and (want to) transform their close bonds, sexual or emotional. Not only do women identify with the emotional content of novels, but they appropriate and rework the text through and in their lives to understand themselves and to make changes in their lives. Lauren Berlant (1995, 2008) and Jacqueline Rose (2005) have emphasized anxiety as the core affect of such a culture of self-improvement, but in my opinion it is a more subtle interplay of anxiety and pleasure produced by real or imagined change that makes self-help culture so powerful.

It is this efferent quality of literature found in women's media genres, such as women's magazines, advice literature, Oprah Winfrey, that make women's emotional—and here sexual—culture so easily translatable into the capitalist market of self-help commodities. Here is one example of such translation:

> In May, Pure Romance [a company teaching intimacy skills] launched their Grey Revolution collection. "We created the gift sets so that anyone could indulge in Grey-inspired fantasies," says Chris Cicchinelli, Pure Romance CEO and president. "Consultants were selling out of fantasy play items like they never had before, most notably products such as whips, floggers and Ben Wa balls, which correspond to scenes from the trilogy." Cicchinelli says they also saw traffic increase to their Fantasy Play page.
>
> Comparing May 2012 through August 2012 to the same timeframe in 2011, bondage sales for Pure Romance have increased 186 percent. In addition, blindfold sales increased 121 percent, their Tie Me Up Tape increased 146 percent, and their Personal Trainer product (Ben Wa balls on a string) increased a staggering 772 percent. (Cooper 2012)

BDSM is thus the center of a narrative formula in which it is in fact a form of sexual self-help, which in turn makes reading *Fifty Shades* a supreme act of modern selfhood: an act of self-empowerment and self-improvement. Self-help has indeed become the core of modern subjectivity, because self-help stands at the juncture between the ideals of autonomy, psychological techniques of self-making, and the vast economic interests of various industries assisting and shaping such process.

Self-help is not only a market segment, it is a whole new modality of culture; that is, it constitutes a new way by which the individual connects to society. Because modernity entails a very large amount of uncertainty about self-worth and the norms and morality that should guide relationships, self-help becomes one of the main pathways for the shaping of selfhood.

To summarize, then: *Fifty Shades of Grey* became a worldwide best-seller because the Internet made it easily accessible, because it resonated with a long tradition of romance, because BDSM, the book's focus, resolved symbolically many of the conundrums of the romantic condition, and finally, because its effect is performative, changing sexual and romantic practices while speaking about them.

CODA / BDSM and Immanence

Let me end with a reflection on the reason the form of BDSM offered in *Fifty Shades of Grey* is highly compatible with self-help as a new cultural mode. Theodor Adorno and Max Horkheimer (1997) viewed the Marquis de Sade as a figure of the Enlightenment and sadomasochism as being at the heart of the modern subject's rationality and moral agency. Relying on a functional interpretation of Immanuel Kant's view of the unity of thought, Adorno and Horkheimer suggested that Kant paved the way for Sade, because Sade's subject is rational, focused on self-preservation, who treats material objects in a mode of pure subjection. The step from Kant to Sade is taken quickly, making Sade's characters caricatural endpoints of the rational subject who treats others in a mode of subjection. Sade reveals that not only is Reason unable to provide a moral guide to behavior, but also that it is the very mechanism that alienates us from the world, from others, and from ourselves. Sade's world reveals the emptiness of Reason and, one may add, of consent itself (for the latter makes sense only if it is based on the former).

In the context that interests me here, I take these remarks to mean something else: I view sadomasochism as belonging to the Enlightenment because it constitutes an immanent solution to the problem of certainty. That is, if modern morality is plagued with the problem of ambivalence (Bauman 1993), uncertainty (Kantola 1994), and indeterminacy (Martine 1992), all resulting from the collapse of an ordered moral cosmos, and if it can no longer ground certainty on a transcendental moral framework, it needs to find immanent solutions to the question of how to ground action on self-generated forms of certainty. BDSM is thus a brilliant fantasy solution to the volatility of romantic relationships, precisely because it is an immanent ritual grounded in a hedonic definition of the subject, providing certainty on roles, pain, the control of pain, and the limits of consent. This is also the very reason that self-help has become the main cultural mode to shape individuality: because it is an immanent solution to the question of how to form a self and how to have worthy relationships and selves. When we cannot ground certainty and self-orientation in rules, norms, or morality, BDSM and self-help become immanent substitutes for it.

Ironically perhaps, such use of literature corresponds to the vocation that philosopher of art Arthur Danto assigns to (highbrow) literature. To quote him:

> Each work of literature shows in this sense an aspect we would not know were ours without benefit of that mirror: each discovers ... an unguessed dimension of the self. It [literature] is a mirror less in passively returning an image than in transforming the self-consciousness of the reader who in virtue of identifying with the image recognizes what he is. Literature is in this sense transfigurative, and in a way cuts across the distinction between fiction and truth. There are metaphors of every life in Herodotus and Gibbon. (1984, 16)

Fifty Shades of Grey is not high literature, but it "cuts across the distinction between fiction and truth" because it brings us to the heart of the contemporary sexual and romantic condition. In that sense, it has the seriousness of those powerful fantasies that help overcome our predicament.

WORKS CITED

Adorno, Theodor, and Max Horkheimer. 1997. *Dialectic of Enlightenment*. Vol. 15. London: Verso.

Arsan, Emmanuelle. 1971. *Emmanuelle*. New York: Grove.

Attwood, Feona. 2005. "What Do People Do with Porn? Qualitative Research into the Consumption, Use, and Experience of Pornography and Other Sexually Explicit Media." *Sexuality and Culture* 9, no. 2.

Barker, Meg, Alessandra Iantaffi, and Camel Gupta. 2008. "Kinky Clients, Kinky Counselling? The Challenges and Potentials of BDSM." In *Feeling Queer or Queer Feelings: Radical Approaches to Counselling Sex, Sexualities and Genders*, edited by Lindsey Moon. London: Routledge.

Bataille, Georges. 1986. *Erotism: Death and Sensuality*. San Francisco: City Lights Books.

Bauman, Zygmunt. 1993. *Modernity and Ambivalence*. London: John Wiley and Sons.

Baumeister, Roy F. 1989. *Masochism and the Self*. Oxford: Psychology Press.

Beck, Ulrich, and Elisabeth Beck-Gernsheim. (1995) 2002. *The Normal Chaos of Love*. Translated by M. Ritter and J. Wiebel. Cambridge: Polity.

Bennett, Jessica. 2008. "The Pornification of a Generation." *Daily Beast*, October 6, accessed November 26, 2012 but since taken down, http://www.thedailybeast.com/newsweek/2008/10/07/the -pornification-of-a-generation.html.

Berlant, Lauren. 1995. "Live Sex Acts." *Feminist Studies* 21, no. 2.

———. 2008. *The Female Complaint: The Unfinished Business of Sentimentality in American Culture.* Durham, NC: Duke University Press.

Booth, Wayne C. 1988. *The Company We Keep: An Ethics of Fiction.* Berkeley: University of California Press.

Bourdieu, Pierre. 1991. *Language and Symbolic Power.* Cambridge, MA: Harvard University Press.

Brand, Roy. 2012. *LoveKnowledge: The Life of Philosophy from Socrates to Derrida.* New York: Columbia University Press.

Brown, Stephen. 2011. "And Then We Come to the Brand: Academic Insights from International Bestsellers." *Arts Marketing: An International Journal* 1, no. 1.

Burzynski, Andrea. 2012. "*Fifty Shades of Grey* Sparks Unexpected Marketing Mania: Publishers and Sex Shops Want to Cash In." *Times of Malta.com,* October 1, accessed November 26, 2012, http://www.timesofmalta.com/articles/view/20121001/books/Fifty-Shades-of-Grey-sparks-unexpected-marketing-mania.439153.

Cantor, Muriel G. 1988. "Feminism and the Media." *Society* 25, no. 5.

Carey, Tanith. 2011. "Why More and More Women Are Using Pornography." *Guardian,* April 7, accessed November 26, 2012, http://www.guardian.co.uk/culture/2011/apr/07/women-addicted-internet-pornography.

Carnes, Mark C., and Clyde Griffen, eds. 1990. *Meanings for Manhood.* Chicago: University of Chicago Press.

Carroll, Bret. 2003. *American Masculinities: A Historical Encyclopedia.* London: Sage.

Cooper, Steve. 2012. "*Fifty Shades* Arouses More Than Book Sales." *Forbes,* September 25, accessed November 27, 2012, http://www.forbes.com/sites/stevecooper/2012/09/25/fifty-shades-arouses-more-than-book-sales/.

Corse, Sarah M., and Saundra Davis Westervelt. 2002. "Gender and Literary Valorization: The Awakening of a Canonical Novel." *Sociological Perspectives* 45, no. 2.

Craigslist. 2008. "Just fucking fuck me, already." *Craigslist,* February 3, accessed November 27, 2012, http://www.craigslist.org/about/best/sea/561877622.html=.

Danto, Arthur C. 1984. "Philosophy as/and/of Literature." *Proceedings and Addresses of the American Philosophical Association* 58, no. 1.

Darnton, Robert. 2009. *The Great Cat Massacre: And Other Episodes in French Cultural History*. New York: Basic Books.

Davis, Natalie Zemon. 1975. *Society and Culture in Early Modern France: Eight Essays*. Palo Alto, CA: Stanford University Press.

Dawkins, Richard. (1976) 2006. *The Selfish Gene*. New York: Oxford University Press.

Defoe, Daniel. (1719) 2012. *Robinson Crusoe*. London: Simon and Brown.

Douglas, Ann. 1980. "Soft-Porn Culture: Punishing the Liberated Woman." *New Republic*, August 30.

Dymock, Alex. 2012. "On the Normalisation of BDSM and the Problem of Pleasure." *Psychology and Sexuality* 3, no. 1 (January).

Eisenstein, Elizabeth L. (1983) 2012. *The Printing Revolution in Early Modern Europe*. New York: Cambridge University Press.

Ellis, Havelock. (1903) 1926. *Studies in the Psychology of Sex*, Vol. 3. Philadelphia: F. A. Davis.

Fein, Ellen, and Sherrie Schneider. (1995) 2007. *All the Rules: Time-Tested Secrets for Capturing the Heart of Mr. Right*. New York: Grand Central.

Fraser, Nancy, and Axel Honneth. 2003. *Redistribution or Recognition? A Philosophical Exchange*. London: Verso.

Freeman, Barbara M. 2001. *The Satellite Sex: The Media and Women's Issues in English Canada, 1966–1971*. Waterloo, Canada: Wilfrid Laurier University Press.

Garlick, Steve. 2011. "Masculinity, Pornography, and the History of Masturbation." *Sexuality and Culture* 16, no. 3.

Giddens, Anthony. 1991. *Modernity and Self-Identity: Self and Society in the Late Modern Age*. Palo Alto, CA: Stanford University Press.

Gilbert, Sandra M., and Susan Gubar. (1979) 2000. *The Madwoman in the Attic: The Woman Writer and the Nineteenth-Century Literary Imagination*. 2nd ed. New Haven, CT: Yale Nota Bene.

Gladwell, Malcolm. (2000) 2003. *The Tipping Point: How Little Things Can Make a Big Difference*. Boston: Little, Brown.

Gray, John. (1992) 2004. *Men Are from Mars, Women Are from Venus: The Classic Guide to Understanding the Opposite Sex*. New York: HarperCollins.

Greer, Germaine. 1994. "Lady, Love Your Cunt." In *The Madwoman's Underclothes: Essays and Occasional Writings*, 74–77. New York: Atlantic Monthly Press

Gross, Daniel. 2006. "Book Clubbed." *Slate,* June 2, accessed November 26, 2012, http://www.slate.com/articles/business/moneybox /2006/06/book_clubbed.html.

Habermas, Jürgen. 1991. *The Structural Transformation of the Public Sphere: An Inquiry into a Category of Bourgeois Society.* Cambridge, MA: MIT Press.

Haldeman-Julius, E. 1928. *The First Hundred Million.* New York: Simon and Schuster.

Harlequin Books. About Us. Accessed November 27, 2012, http:// www.harlequinbooks.com.au/about.

Harris, Tami W. 2012. "*Clutch* Book Club: *50 Shades of Grey.*" *Clutch,* May 31, accessed November 27, 2012, http://www.clutchmagonline .com/2012/05/clutch-book-club-50-shades-of-grey/.

Harvey, J. 1953. "The Content Characteristics of Best-Selling Novels." *Public Opinion Quarterly* 17, no. 1.

Hayden, Dorothy C. 2012. "Psychological Surrender," *Revise F65,* accessed November 27, 2012, http://www.revisef65.org/hayden2 .html.

Hays, Sharon. 1996. *The Cultural Contradictions of Motherhood.* New Haven, CT: Yale University Press.

Hicks, G. 1934. "The Mystery of the Best Seller." *English Journal* 23 (October).

Hunt, Lynn A. 1991. *Eroticism and the Body Politic.* Baltimore: Johns Hopkins University Press.

Illouz, Eva. 2003. *Oprah Winfrey and the Glamour of Misery: An Essay on Popular Culture.* New York: Columbia University Press.

————. 2012. *Why Love Hurts.* Cambridge: Polity Press.

James, E. L. 2012. *Fifty Shades of Grey.* New York: Vintage.

————. 2012. *Fifty Shades Darker* (vol. 2 of the trilogy). New York: Vintage.

————. 2012. *Fifty Shades Freed* (vol. 3 of the trilogy). New York: Vintage.

James, Susan D. 2012. "50 Shades of Grey: Why 'Mommy Porn' Is Hot." *ABC News,* April 3, accessed November 26, 2012, http:// abcnews.go.com/Health/50-shades-grey-women-turned-sexual -submission/story?id=16059118.

Jameson, Fredric. 1975. "Magical Narratives: Romance as Genre." *New Literary History* 7, no. 1.

Janus, Samuel S., and Cynthia L. Janus. 1994. *Report on Sexual Behavior.* London: John Wiley and Sons.

Kantola, Ilkka. 1994. *Probability and Moral Uncertainty in Late Medieval and Early Modern Times.* Helsinki: University of Helsinki, Luther-Agricola Society.

Kate, Roddy E. 2011. "Masochist or Machiavel? Reading Harley Quinn in Canon and Fanon." *Transformative Works and Cultures* 8.

Laplanche, Jean, and Jean-Bertrand Pontalis. 1974. *The Language of Psycholoanalysis.* New York: W. W. Norton.

Laumann, Edward O., John H. Gagnon, Robert T. Michael, and Stuart Michaels. (1994) 2000. *The Social Organization of Sexuality: Sexual Practices in the United States.* Chicago: University of Chicago Press.

Linden, Dana W., and Matt Rees. 1992. "I'm Hungry. But Not for Food." *Forbes* 150 (July 6).

Liner, Elaine. 2012. "Eat, Screw, Love: *50 Shades of Grey* Is 'Mommy Porn' You Don't Have to Hide." *Dallas Observer: Blogs*, March 22, accessed November 26, 2012, http://blogs.dallasobserver.com /mixmaster/2012/03/50_shades_of_grey_were.php.

Loach, Loretta. 1992. "Bad Girls: Women Who Use Pornography." In *Sex Exposed: Sexuality and the Pornography Debate*, edited by L. Segal and M. Macintosh. London: Virago.

Long, Elizabeth. 1992. "Textual Interpretation as Collective Action." *Discourse* 14, no. 3.

Longhofer, Wesley, Shannon Golden, and Arturo Baiocchi. 2010. "A Fresh Look at Sociology Bestsellers." *Contexts* 9, no. 2.

Martine, Brian John. 1992. *Indeterminacy and Intelligibility.* Albany: State University of New York Press.

Massé, Michelle A. 1992. *In the Name of Love: Women, Masochism, and the Gothic.* Ithaca, NY: Cornell University Press.

Masters, William H., Virginia E. Johnson, and Robert C. Kolodny. 1995. *Human Sexuality.* New York: HarperCollins.

May, Simon. 2011. *Love: A History.* New Haven, CT: Yale University Press.

McRobbie, Angela. 1991. *Feminism and Youth Culture: From "Jackie" to "Just Seventeen."* London: Macmillan.

Müller, Julian, and Victoria von Groddeck. n.d. Working paper. University of Munich, Institute of Sociology.

National Coalition for Sexual Freedom. n.d. "How Many People En-

gage in SM?" Accessed November 27, 2012, https://ncsfreedom
.org/key-programs/consent-counts/consent-counts/item/364
-what-is-sm-how-many-people-engage-in-sm?.html=.

Nehring, Cristina. 2009. *A Vindication of Love: Reclaiming Romance for the Twenty-First Century*. New York: Harper.

North, Anna. 2012. "Why Women Really Like '50 Shades Of Grey': It's about Being Served."*BuzzFeed*, June 6, accessed November 26, 2012, http://www.buzzfeed.com/annanorth/why-50-shades-of-grey-is-less-about-submission-a.

Norwood, Robin. 2008. *Women Who Love Too Much*. New York: Simon and Schuster.

Parks, Tim. 2012. "Does Copyright Matter?" *NYRblog*, August 14, accessed November 26, 2012, http://www.nybooks.com/blogs/nyrblog/2012/aug/14/does-copyright-matter/.

Pringle, Edward J. 1853. *Slavery in the Southern States*. Cambridge, MA: John Bartlett.

Radway, Janice. 1997. *A Feeling for Books: The Book-of-the-Month Club, Literary Taste, and Middle-Class Desire*. Chapel Hill: University of North Carolina Press.

Réage, Pauline. (1954) 2012. *Story of O*. London: Transworld.

Regis, Pamela. 2011. *A Natural History of the Romance Novel*. Philadelphia: University of Pennsylvania Press.

Reinisch, June M., and Ruth Beasley. 1990. *The Kinsey Institute New Report on Sex: What You Must Know to Be Sexually Literate*. New York: St. Martin's.

Richardson, Samuel. (1740) 2001. *Pamela: Or Virtue Rewarded*. Oxford: Oxford University Press.

Roiphe, Katie. 2012. "Spanking Goes Mainstream." *Daily Beast*, April 16, accessed November 27, 2012, http://www.thedailybeast.com/newsweek/2012/04/15/working-women-s-fantasies.html.

Romance Writers of America. "The Romance Genre" and "Industry Statistics." Accessed November 27, 2012, http://www.rwa.org/cs/the_romance_genre/romance_literature_statistics/industry_statistics.

Rose, Jacqueline. 2005. *Sexuality in the Field of Vision*. London: Verso.

Rosenblatt, Louise. 1987. "Efferent and Aesthetic Transactions." In *English Literature in Schools*, edited by V. J. Lee. Milton Keynes, UK: Open University Press.

Rutter, Virginia, and Pepper Schwartz. 2011. *The Gender of Sexuality: Exploring Sexual Possibilities*. Washington, DC: Rowman and Littlefield.

Schiffrin, André. 2001. *The Business of Books: How International Conglomerates Took Over Publishing and Changed the Way We Read*. London: Verso.

Schudson, Michael. 1989. "How Culture Works: Perspectives from Media Studies on the Efficacy of Symbols." *Theory and Society* 18, no. 2.

Scruton, Roger. 2006. *Sexual Desire: A Philosophical Investigation*. London: Continuum International.

Shipside, Steve. 2008. *Samuel Smiles' Self-Help: A 52 Brilliant Ideas Interpretation*. Oxford: Infinite Ideas.

Siegel, Tatiana. 2012. "'Fifty Shades of Grey' Movie Producers Considering Surprising Screenwriters (Exclusive)." *Hollywood Reporter*, July 8, accessed November 26, 2012, http://www.hollywoodreporter.com/news/fifty-shades-grey-producers-screenwriters-359080.

Snitow, Ann B., Christine Stansell, and Sharon Thompson, eds. 1983. *Powers of Desire: The Politics of Sexuality*. New York: Monthly Review Press.

Tegarden, Diane. 2004. *Getting OUT of Limbo: A Self Help Divorce Book for Women*. Pasadena: FireWalker.

Thoele, Sue Patton. 2001. *The Courage to Be Yourself: A Woman's Guide to Emotional Strength and Self-Esteem*. Boston: Conari.

Thomas, Calvin. 2009. "On Being Post-normal: Heterosexuality after Queer Theory." In *The Ashgate Research Companion to Queer Theory*, edited by Noreen Giffney and Michael O'Rourke. Surrey, UK: Ashgate.

Thurston, Carol. 1987. *The Romance Revolution: Erotic Novels for Women and the Quest for a New Sexual Identity*. Champaign: University of Illinois Press.

Tompkins, Jane P. 1986. *Sensational Designs: The Cultural Work of American Fiction, 1790–1860*. New York: Oxford University Press.

Verboord, M. 2011. "Market Logic and Cultural Consecration in French, German, and American Bestseller Lists, 1970–2007." *Poetics* 39, no. 4.

Watt, Ian. (1957) 2001. *The Rise of the Novel: Studies in Defoe, Richardson, and Fielding*. Berkeley: University of California Press.

Weeks, E. 1936. "What Makes a Book a Best Seller?" *New York Times Book Review*, December 20.

Weinberg, Thomas S. 2006. "Sadomasochism and the Social Sciences." *Journal of Homosexuality* 50, nos. 2–3.

Williams, Linda. 1989. *Hard Core: Power, Pleasure, and the "Frenzy of the Visible."* Berkeley: University of California Press.

Williams, Raymond. 1975. *The Country and the City.* New York: Oxford University Press.

INDEX